INSIDE
CORPORATE INNOVATION

*Strategy, Structure,
and Managerial Skills*

ROBERT A. BURGELMAN
LEONARD R. SAYLES

THE FREE PRESS
A Division of Macmillan, Inc.
NEW YORK

For Rita and Stefan and Oliver—R.A.B.

The Free Press
A Division of Macmillan, Inc.
866 Third Avenue, New York, N.Y. 10022

First Free Press Paperback Edition 1988

Printed in the United States of America

printing number
2 3 4 5 6 7 8 9 10

Library of Congress Cataloging in Publication Data

Burgelman, Robert A.
   Inside corporate innovation.

   Includes index.
   1. Technological innovations—Management.   2. New
products.   I. Sayles, Leonard R.   II. Title.   III. Title:
Corporate innovation.
HD45.B798   1986   658.4   85-15846
ISBN 0-02-904341-7

Contents

Preface

"It was the big play that paid off," Bradshaw said. "When you were be-hind," he was asked, "did you tell yourself the big play would come?" "No. Big plays happen on their own. I never saw a big play that was designed. They just happen."[1]

But what makes some see the upcoming "big play"? What makes some capable of grabbing it, while others fumble? What are the differences between a process that leads to the "big play" and one that doesn't?

In this book, our concern is with the description and analysis of the behaviors of managers in large, established firms trying for the "big play," that is, in firms that are trying to define new opportunities and develop new structures for doing business in areas beyond their current corporate field of operations.

In the late 1970s, some were pointing at the lagging innovative capability of American industry, while others were suggesting the existence of a tradeoff between productivity and innovation, and still others were predicting the extinction of the "entrepreneur" in a corporate environment that was becoming increasingly stifling and in an increasingly regulated economic environment. In this climate, it seemed like a hazardous undertaking to do a study of the process of "corporate entrepreneurship" and to document the role of entrepreneurial individuals in the large corporation.

In 1985, this task seems less hazardous but by no means less important. To be sure, there has been a major revival in the area of venture capital investment and the formation of new high-tech firms. However, many large, established firms, and even some of the best-managed ones, are still struggling to get on a new course of real growth through internal development.[2]

Therefore, we hope our efforts to shed more light on fundamental and lasting phenomena involved in the innovation process of such firms will be relevant and helpful to top-, middle-, and operational-level managers who are trying to engage in strategic renewal.

The processes we document turned out to be rather complex, and the following chapters reflect this. But we think that the reader will agree, after reading this book, that, even though it may not be possible to design the "big play" in corporate entrepreneurship, we are able to provide more insight into this phenomenon than to simply say that "they just happen." We do so by providing a very detailed view of how all the relevant players not only behave, but change their behavior over the extended time required to convert a new idea into a major new venture for the corporation.

Acknowledgments

This book exists because of the cooperation of the people at "United Corporation." Confronted with an open-ended research proposal, they were nevertheless prepared to let an outsider scrutinize some of their most intimate strategic decisions. More than 60 very busy executives and scientists made time available to share their work experiences and their views regarding internal corporate venturing. Because of their openness, they and their corporation must remain anonymous. This book is our thanks to them.

The research for our book began as a dissertation by Burgelman, with Sayles as his advisor. We felt that we could fruitfully blend some of Sayles's work with some of Burgelman's findings and conceptualizations, and write a research-based book that would appeal not only to academics but also to managers searching for a framework by which to understand the complexities and subtleties involved in managing corporate entrepreneurship, innovation, and venturing. This book is the result of our joint efforts over five years.

Since 1981, Burgelman has received the support of the Strategic Management Program of Stanford University's Graduate School of

Business. His colleagues L. Jay Bourgeois, III, David B. Jemison, and Steven C. Wheelwright were generous with their helpful comments on various journal articles that formed the basis for chapters in the book.

Sayles wishes to express his appreciation to the Center for Research in Career Development at Columbia's Graduate School of Business. They provided financial aid for two summers of writing.

Both authors wish to express their appreciation to Robert Wallace, our Free Press editor, who manages to combine enthusiasm, persistence, and patience with an unusual knowledge of the field.

A special thanks from Burgelman goes to Stanford's Jeannette Ochoa, who has diligently entered numerous drafts and even more "minor changes" on the word processor. Her friendly willingness to put up with an author's sense of urgency has helped make the venture a more pleasant one. Sayles, as with previous books, had the extraordinarily good fortune of working with Ms. Joy Glazener, a secretary without equal.

Finally, a word of thanks from Burgelman to Rita and their sons Stefan and Oliver. All three have been wise enough to go about their business and leave him to his writing. They never seemed to doubt that the book would be finished one day or that work would just go on afterwards.

CHAPTER 1

Internal Corporate Venturing
Innovation and Entrepreneurship in Established Firms

Major changes have taken place in American business during the last 20 years. Self-confidence based on a position of great prestige in the world economy, a sense of being the "best and the brightest," has given way to a position characterized by self-doubt and defensiveness. After World War II, and throughout the 1950s and 1960s, European and Japanese managers trooped dutifully to the United States to visit its corporations and business schools, in order to learn the secrets of success of American business. Many American corporations were seen as invincible leaders in technology, marketing, and organization. For some European observers, the "American challenge"[1] represented a crucial event, requiring fundamental changes in the ways of doing business on the part of the Europeans in order to be able to respond. For other observers, the preeminence of American business was simply viewed as threatening the autonomy and economic welfare of Western Europe if not the rest of the world.

During the 1970s, the tables turned dramatically,[2] and during the first half of the 1980s, the theme of "Managing Our Way to Economic Decline"[3] has dominated the headlines in the American busi-

1

ness press. American management has been seeking to catch up and learn new skills and new approaches to both new and traditional problems related to managing large, complex business organizations. Among the criticisms that have stung American executives are accusations that their organizations are bureaucratic, inadequately innovative, too slow to adapt, and inflexible. At the same time, critics have argued that the capacity of these organizations to efficiently manufacture high-quality goods has also greatly diminished.

The New Industrial Context

It would, of course, be naive to propose that the relative decline of some parts of American business is solely due to ineptitude on the part of managers of established firms. At least three other major sets of forces should be considered when attempting to diagnose the relative decline.

First, and perhaps most important, major shifts in relative comparative advantage in factors of production may underlay a good deal of the problems encountered by basic American industries. Reich,[4] for instance, has cogently argued that American comparative advantage may lie in more quick-changing, customized product and technology development, rather than in the highly routinized, mature industries where relative labor cost disadvantages can no longer be overcome by capital improvements. The fact that Japan currently experiences similar pressures as a result of Korean and Taiwanese competition in certain areas may underscore this point.

Second, as the research of Abernathy and Utterback has suggested,[5] some of the setbacks of organizations may be the result of the very logic of technological development: The forces driving the exploitation of existing technological opportunities structurally impede the development of new ones. The classic example is, of course, the American automobile industry.[6] Hence, the large aggregations of people and capital represented by the traditional large firms may do well enough, even superbly, when mass production, strict routines, and tightly controlled procedures can be used to attack relatively stable and very large markets. The emphasis of such organizations is, most naturally, on process innovation and improved manufacturing capabilities, not on new-product development.

Third, many observers agree that the technological foundations

2

for many of the high-flying industries of the 1950s and 1960s are now being replaced by new ones—electronics and biotechnology being the most salient examples—and that fresh and different approaches are required to develop the new entrepreneurial opportunities offered by these new technologies. Emphasis on new-product development and fast-moving strategic positioning and repositioning is essential here. Not surprisingly, *new* firms have been more adept at performing the entrepreneurial function than established ones. As a result of the "Silicon Valley" effect, entirely new geographic areas are emerging as loci of industrial development.

American industry shows great vigor in these new areas of technology. New-firm formation has been rather spectacular, stimulated in part by the enormous influx of venture capital that occurred after the capital gains tax changes of 1978. Established firms, however, continue to struggle to find management approaches for returning to real growth derived from internal development rather than from acquisitions.[7]

Some Proposed Solutions

Corresponding to these major shifts in the industrial and organizational environments and the recognition of significant managerial shortcomings, various solutions and approaches have recently been proposed.

Some scholars have focused on the problems of industry maturity and the competitiveness of manufacturers. Abernathy and associates[8] have made a useful study of the concept of "de-maturity," or the possibility of changing industry dynamics to a point where product technology and innovation can again become tools for creating a competitive advantage. Some recent changes in the automobile industry, for instance, seem to provide a basis for believing that such an "industrial renaissance" is possible. Recognizing the difficulties of bringing about massive change in established organizations, General Motors has proposed utilizing a newly created, completely autonomous division to produce its new "Saturn" subcompact. By so doing it hopes to protect the required new technologies and work methods from being diluted by existing management routines and procedures. A major element in "de-maturity" concerns improving competitiveness in the area of operations and manufacturing management. As

3

Hayes and Wheelwright[9] have recently suggested, this will require in many cases the full integration of considerations related to operations and manufacturing at the highest levels of firms' strategic management.

Other scholars have focused on the broader learning and adaptation capacities of established organizations. Lawrence and Dyer,[10] for instance, present an elaborate discussion of organizational renewal, including recommendations for management-union and management-government relations, geared toward making organizations both efficient and innovative. Ouchi[11] has made a strong plea for enlightened teamwork at the interorganizational level, drawing on some lessons from Japanese as well as American firms (e.g., Hewlett-Packard) that have effectively combined hierarchical, market, and clan-type elements in their management process (clan-type arrangements being based on long-term relationships of mutual aid and sharing and the expectation that all will share equitably in any gain—in contrast to short-term, individualized incentives).

Peters and Waterman[12] have documented some of the approaches used by consistently high-performing U.S. companies. Some of these authors' recommendations center around the importance of encouraging individuals to experiment, the utilization of "skunk works" (i.e., small groups of zealots working "under the table"), and the capacity of the organization to operate while involved in a continuous learning process. Kanter[13] documents the important role played by middle managers who can initiate both laterally and upward to create change in spite of bureaucratic impediments. Kanter describes the individuals who effectively create change within firms as hard-driving persons who possess an astute awareness of organizational politics, while Peters and Waterman urge top management personnel to effect change by "hanging loose." These two views are in sensible opposition to the now-dated picture of a small number of wise top managers controlling, with some precision, the activities of docile and less-able followers, and thus imposing change from above.[14]

The Lure of the "Quick Fix"

The natural reaction of companies faced with a new challenge is to seek one-step, well-packaged solutions or "fixes" that look most attractive (and have received wide publicity) and that can be grafted onto the organization with the least trouble, or so it seems. In earlier days, corporations sought to train their staff to be more creative and to manage their research and development (R&D) efforts better (which usually meant making them more cost-efficient). During the 1960s and early 1970s, the creation of separate new-venture groups seemed to be the answer to the problem of creating truly new businesses in the corporate context. This had become almost faddish, and when a recession struck in the mid-1970s, many such groups were abandoned.[15] Today the "eight lessons" of *In Search of Excellence* are sometimes naively embraced as the new "quick fix." [Excellent companies presumably distinguish themselves by]

1. Having a bias for action
2. Being close to the customer
3. Fostering autonomy and entrepreneurship
4. Seeking productivity through people
5. Being hands-on, value-driven
6. Sticking to their knitting
7. Having a simple form, a lean staff
8. Having simultaneously loose–tight properties

As an article in *Business Week*[16] recently observed, however, "excellence" is a transient phenomenon in many cases. Some companies that are no longer excellent didn't continue to adhere, it seems, to the eight lessons. More disturbing is the fact that some firms are no longer excellent even though they *did* adhere to them.

What this suggests, we believe, is that even though "quick fixes" may often contain significant elements of truth, they usually fail because they are not based on an understanding of how organizations work and the processes of change. Since sensible business leadership often seems so easy and the stories told to demonstrate how effective leaders function seem so convincing, it is important to ask why so many companies fail to be well managed, to be both innovative and productive. Obviously the answer must be that there is much more to rejuvenating an organization and obtaining a fresh flow of new-business development than, for instance, simply utilizing a "skunk works" or a new-venture group.

These conditions motivated us to undertake the more onerous task of trying to observe and document the actions and motives of the key players in a management system and seeking to understand the process by which forces leading to change work their way through a whole series of organizational barriers before they become realized. We also perceived the need to develop a *theoretical framework* showing the complex (but manageable) set of managerial choices and processes that must be meticulously maneuvered and manipulated if innovations are to be created in the laboratory and moved through the many required stages of elaboration that can result in the creation of a commercially successful new product and, eventually, in the existence of a free-standing new-business division for the corporation.

A Study of the Internal Corporate Venturing Process

The scholars whose work we have discussed in the preceding section have attempted to develop theoretical frameworks derived from careful interpretation of data. What we feel has been lacking, however, and where we hope to make a contribution with this book, is to develop an all-encompassing view of how a total organization works when it is seeking to develop major new business activities based on new technologies.

Thus, several years ago we began a research project to examine what we thought were some of the most critical questions regarding the management *process* involved in the efforts of large, established firms to be innovative. In the Appendix to this book, entitled "Methodology and Research Design," we have explained in some detail how we went about doing the study, but here we want to sketch briefly the essence of what we have tried to do.

We were, of course, aware that many U.S. corporations, like AT&T, 3M, and DuPont, had learned to nurture and commercialize major innovations, and we sought to review what was known about their successes. However, our major efforts were concentrated on a longitudinal study of one major corporation in the multi-billion-dollar class with a major commitment to R&D.

We had the opportunity to look at what could be called a "most difficult case" situation. The term does not mean that we were looking at a near-bankrupt or inept company, but rather that we could examine how a very large, truly massive corporation with major commitments and most of its experience in more routinized, large-scale production and commodities marketing used its enormous capabili-

6

ties and resources to branch out into really new areas of technology and markets.

We called these "radical innovations"—from the perspective of the corporation—because they were not the usual modifications and improvements of existing product lines, but rather represented efforts to move into new industries, to try out new technologies, and to market entirely new products. These efforts could not draw much on the existing corporate know-how and culture, even though the origins of these efforts emerged from internal development efforts. They also required that new administrative units be created to oversee these activities, and these new units would have to be integrated into the overall corporate structure when they reached sufficient maturity.

It was this situation, we felt, that represented the most difficult test of managerial skills and processes and would allow us to examine how such efforts interact with existing corporate strategy and structure. Furthermore, we considered that such radical innovation was not oddball or trivial, precisely because many established firms are now being faced with increasing their capacity to engage in such *strategic* renewal.

Our objective was to "tease out" the underlying and often hidden organizational events and managerial behaviors that are associated with successful new-business development, as well as to highlight the pitfalls awaiting the unwary or naive. In so doing, we have recognized that the large modern corporation has many features potentially advantageous to innovation, which we will highlight in this book.

As might be expected, the great challenge of successful innovation could not simply be met by a single organizational solution (such as establishment of a new-venture group) or by calling for more "entrepreneurship" on the part of employees. Rather, as we looked systematically and over time at how new ideas jelled in R&D and began to grow into fledgling new ventures, we observed how truly complex were the organizational and leadership requirements for this process to take place. There were countless ways in which new ideas could get distorted, bottled up, or fail to be property elaborated and integrated with marketing and manufacturing requirements (among others). Not surprisingly, failure is more probable than success in initiating new-business ventures. There were literally dozens of critical events that had to be worked out right and come together at the right time in order to effectively build a viable new business based on new technology.

In the following chapters, we seek to describe and conceptualize the "how-to-do-it" aspect in terms of the activities that are required of managers and professionals in the various stages of the process that begins in the laboratory and culminates in the existence of the successful, independent new division. We will highlight the traps and dilemmas that managers experience all along the tortuous way, and document how they cope or fail to cope with them. Before we do this, however, it is useful to situate our study in the research literature on internal corporate venturing (ICV).

Research on Internal Corporate Venturing

Research interest in ICV is relatively new.[17] Early contributions came from practitioners of ICV who described their firm's approach and provided anecdotal observations regarding *practices* in such corporations as 3M,[18] Owens-Illinois,[19] and DuPont.[20] More systematic research[21] led to the reporting of survey results regarding ICV management practices and to the description of characteristics varying from educational background of the venture manager to the parent firm's reasons for introducing new-venture management.

One major research study of ICV was done by Eric von Hippel.[22] He collected data by means of face-to-face interviews with different levels of venture management and key staff, using a structured interview guide. Financial data were obtained from venture records. Von Hippel found many different forms of implementation of the venture concept, but identified two features that were invariably present in his sample: (1) the existence of a "venture manager"—the chief executive officer (CEO) of the venture—and (2) the existence of a "venture sponsor," the executive to whom the venture manager reported. The latter provided funding and formal hierarchical linkage between the venture and the parent corporation. In addition, he found that venture management is being practiced in many different areas of business and can at least potentially succeed or fail in all of these. He also found that there is a strong relationship between venture success and the prior experience of the parent corporation and/or the venturing personnel with the customers addressed by the given venture;

that there is no significant correlation between the distance of venture sponsor to corporate CEO and the success of the venture; and that chances of failure seem to be higher if the venture manager comes from a previous position in which he or she managed a greater amount of resources than that involved in the venture.

A second major research study was done by Ralph Biggadike.[23] Based on a sample from the top 200 firms of the *Fortune* 500 and data from Profit Impact of Market Strategies (PIMS) project, Biggadike found that it takes an average of 10 to 12 years before the return on investment (ROI) of new ventures equals that of mature businesses. He found that rapid share building—at the expense of current financial performance—is a key element in venture success, and thus advises large-scale entry for a limited number of ventures as the most adequate strategy for new business development. "Launching new businesses," he says, "takes large entry scale and continual commitment; it is not an activity for the impatient or for the faint-hearted."

A third major research study was carried out by Norman Fast.[24] Fast's research has focused on the "new-venture division" (NVD) level of analysis. Based on a survey of 18 companies that had NVDs at some point between 1965 and 1975, and on three in-depth case studies, Fast found that NVDs not only took on diverse shapes, but also that a high proportion of them were short-lived. Of the 18 NVDs studied 9 were inoperative by 1976. These had an average life-span of only 4 years. Of eleven NVDs established before 1970, seven were inoperative by 1976. Furthermore, Fast found that NVDs become inoperative in one of three ways: (1) by retaining the ventures they had started and growing into an operating division, (2) by being given a staff function, and (3) by being disbanded. He noted that most of the surviving NVDs also evolved through the course of their development, and that the driving forces behind such evolution were: (1) changes in the corporate strategic posture and (2) changes in the NVD's political posture. Fast's research thus indicated clearly the need to study further the ICV activities in the context of the overall corporate strategic process.

Some Remaining Issues

The earlier studies have revealed a number of problems pertaining to the management of ICV. They also have identified key tasks and roles, and certain traits that successful occupants of these roles seem to possess. The review of past studies, however, reveals a number of missing elements in our understanding.[25]

First, the study of ICV has not focused systematically on the transformation of "inventions" into "innovations," which is one of the key problems in today's large high-technology corporations.[26] *Invention* refers to a company's seeking technical perfection and allied new ways of production as ends in themselves. *Innovation* refers to a company's efforts in instituting new methods of production and/or bringing new products or services to market. The criteria of success are "technical" for invention, but "commercial" for innovation. The link between invention and innovation is the "entrepreneurial" capability of an individual and/or an organization. ICV typically involves both invention and innovation and requires entrepreneurial ability.

Second, the limitation of past research to the study of ICV development up to the "first commercialization" stage has led to a situation where one of the major stages—the development of an "embryonic" business into a "mature" one in the context of a corporate structure—has been incompletely documented. This is the stage where the role of entrepreneurial activities is most strongly manifest. Numerous publications exist that deal with the role of the entrepreneur in the large corporation.[27] However, no systematic studies exist that document the behavior of such individuals step by step and elucidate the contradiction between these behaviors and their rationale and certain routines and expectations in the broader corporate context. In addition, the research we have cited has primarily focused on the individual entrepreneur rather than on the relationship of the role of the individual entrepreneur to the broader concept of "corporate entrepreneurship."

Past studies have insufficiently documented the ways in which specific tasks and roles interact in the invention-innovation process, how these interactions may change from stage to stage, and what the problems are that are correlated with these shifts. One of the authors of this book[28] pointed out that the stages in the invention-innovation process do not form a neat sequential process, and are not independent of one another. Most academic research has focused on the end points of the process: the "inception" (getting good ideas) and the "application" (getting the user to accept the new product). Yet, the more difficult and more critical management problems appear to occur in the middle, in the linkages that tie together all the substages between inception and application. In these intermediate linkages, the management of the interface between R&D and business people is crucial and problematic. Recent studies have repeatedly indicated that the quality of the working relationships and of the communication between these two groups is a major determinant of the chances of successful innovation.[29]

Past studies have also insufficiently recognized that ICV development is a complex "organizational" strategic decision-making process. The ICV process is spread over multiple levels of management and is subject to forces in the corporate context which it can, however, also partially influence.[30] Many decisions and events take place at these multiple levels that affect the developmental course of an ICV project. These events and decisions often take place simultaneously and sometimes even in reverse order to what a typical sequential innovation process would suggest.

Finally, past studies have also insufficiently focused on the generic problems that result from the simultaneous existence of the operating divisions (the "mainstream") and the ICV activities in the corporate context, and the fact that these two different areas may interfere with each other. Figure 1–1 depicts the structure of the corporation that we studied in depth, and allows us to visualize better this category of issues and problems.

Figure 1–1 depicts what we call the "operating system" of the corporation: the set of operating divisions that cover the "current domain" and the "related diversification" efforts associated with the corporate strategy. It also shows the new-venture division that covers the "unrelated diversification" areas. Because the activities of the operating system and the new-venture division are seldom completely independent of each other, tricky areas of interdependence often arise which create complex management problems relating to how to make the interface between these two domains successful.

The Purpose of Our Process Study

The purpose of our study is to build on the past research studies and to provide some additional insights in the areas that remained relatively unexplored.

Our study is a process study of the organizational decision-making process regarding ICV, and it encompasses various levels of analysis. We shall document the entire developmental cycle of new

Figure 1-1

The Structure of United Corporation (*Reprinted from "A Process Model of Internal Corporate Venturing in the Diversified Major Firm" by R. A. Burgelman published in* Administrative Science Quarterly, *June 1983, by permission of* The Administrative Science Quarterly. *Copyright 1983 Cornell University.*)

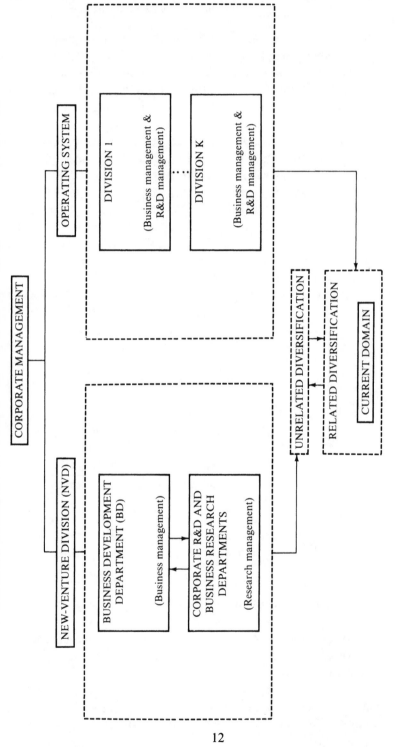

ventures, which as pointed out earlier may take more than a dozen years. We want to elucidate the transformation of invention into innovation, ranging from a discussion of R&D experiments through staged approvals, pilot plant decisions, commercialization efforts, to the attainment of divisional status by the new venture. We will document the entrepreneurial activities of different managers in the various stages of the development, indicate how these activities interlock with each other, and show how the interfaces between different functional groups shift as the new venture moves through the different stages of development. We also want to discuss the issues and problems associated with establishing a separate new-venture division.

At one level, we will be discussing the "evolving constraints," which change through the development cycle and which comprise such elements as user requirements and demands; the achievement of technical feasibility, marketability, and reasonable cost; external related technological developments; the actions of competitors; changing corporate profitability, "slack," and interests; and other changing environmental forces.

At another level, we will be discussing the relatively "fixed constraints" within which the developmental cycle unfolds. These include such elements as corporate culture, values, and strategic orientations; interdivisional competitiveness; and functional technical criteria applied by the various groups that get involved in the process. Figure 1–2 shows the two levels that our discussion will address.

Audience

Who then are we writing for? One audience we have kept in mind is senior executives interested in improving the ability of their organizations to generate real innovation. Obviously those upper- and middle-level managers directly responsible for evaluating and nurturing new products should also find this material relevant to their day-to-day managerial responsibilities. In most businesses of any size, commercial managers have to deal with their technical counterparts both in obtaining technological and manufacturing inputs and, on some occasions, in having to prepare for the potential development and transfer of products resulting from new technological advances. Often their efforts to coordinate events and bridge the cultural gap that separates the technically trained from the business trained are

Figure 1-2
A Case Study of New-Venture Development
Decision-Making Developmental "Cycle"

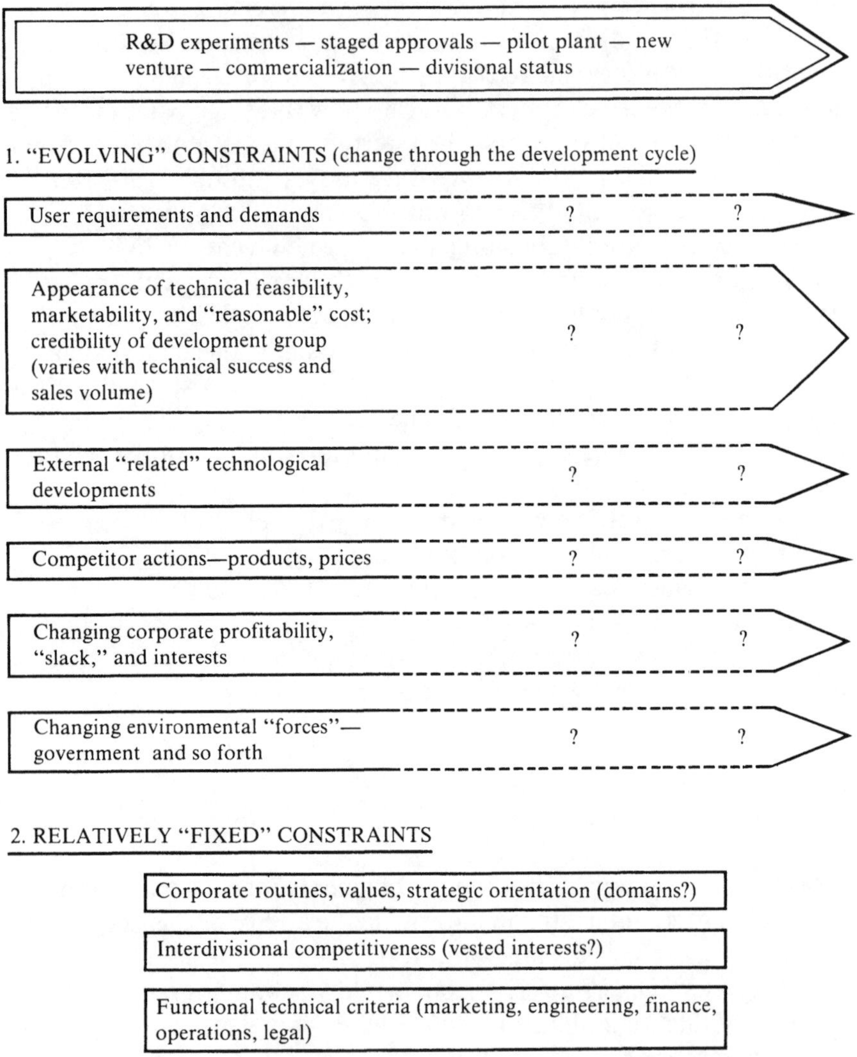

R&D experiments — staged approvals — pilot plant — new
venture — commercialization — divisional status

1. "EVOLVING" CONSTRAINTS (change through the development cycle)

User requirements and demands   ?   ?

Appearance of technical feasibility,
marketability, and "reasonable" cost;
credibility of development group   ?   ?
(varies with technical success and
sales volume)

External "related" technological   ?   ?
developments

Competitor actions—products, prices   ?   ?

Changing corporate profitability,   ?   ?
"slack," and interests

Changing environmental "forces"—   ?   ?
government and so forth

2. RELATIVELY "FIXED" CONSTRAINTS

Corporate routines, values, strategic orientation (domains?)

Interdivisional competitiveness (vested interests?)

Functional technical criteria (marketing, engineering, finance,
operations, legal)

exacerbated by a less-than-realistic view of how new technologically
based products come "into the world." A more realistic understanding of the high-risk, complicated route by which a R&D idea gets
"developed" into a new product should improve their capabilities to
communicate and coordinate effectively.

While our book has been written with maximal emphasis on straightforward description of the innovation process and the development cycle, we think the findings will be of relevance to our academic colleagues who teach and do research on new-product development, innovation, and R&D management. We have sought to provide a first-hand account using data derived from actual experience of a complex organizational process that we believe has rarely been observed systematically. We think this carefully documented, more "sociological" view of the process of corporate innovation should be a useful addition to the literature on the management of modern business organizations.

Overview of the Book

In summary, this is a book concerned with the management of new technologies, with innovation, and with corporate entrepreneurship. We think its unique contribution is that it looks at all these factors in the context of the day-to-day life of a large corporation. Our method stresses *how* and *when* events occur and *who* is involved. It is this managerial process that enables one executive or one company to learn from another in contrast to being told that this or that technique will accomplish great things—what we have earlier termed the "quick fix."

In the following chapters, we present our findings, theory-building efforts, and recommendations. We start with a discussion of corporate R&D management (Chapter 2), which is a major source for generating ideas for new-business development. In Chapters 3 through 7 we discuss the major stages in the developmental process of a new venture, and the problems emerging in the interfaces between technical and business people in the definition and development of a new business venture. Chapter 8 presents our findings on the difficulties generated and encountered by the existence of a new-venture group within a corporation.

Chapter 9 is the core chapter of the book. It provides a reconceptualization of our findings at the project and corporate levels of analysis, and combines them in a new model of ICV as a strategic process.

Chapter 10 presents recommendations for making the ICV strategy work better. In Chapter 11, our final chapter, we propose a more general framework concerning corporate entrepreneurship and examine an array of organization designs—over and beyond the NVD design—for facilitating the strategic management of corporate entrepreneurship.

CHAPTER 2

Can Exploratory Research Be Planned?

A classic problem for industrial R&D is the setting of goals and directions. There is an inevitable tension between the need of the organization for tangible, commercially profitable results and the need of science to make advances in knowledge. In theory, the scientists in industry, guided by the canons of science, seek to make intellectual breakthroughs (which will lead to publishable results) and to remain autonomous from "lay" administrators who are likely to have unrealistically short time limits and little awareness of how and where scientific advance is possible or likely.

For their part, administrators have come to be suspicious of the impartiality and scientific judgment of the professional. They recognize that scientists too have their blinders and their vested interests. Kuhn documented, for example, how the most prestigious nuclear physicists misled companies seeking to pioneer in commercializing nuclear energy by recommending development of a very technologically advanced breeder reactor some decades ago.[1] The commercial potential of many interesting scientific discoveries can be developed only if one has extraordinary patience. Thus, the so-called amorphous metals were "discovered" in the 1960s but their commercial applications have been slow in developing. (In contrast, lasers, which also seemed largely a laboratory curiosity, have found extensive commercial applications.)

It is not surprising that management insists on careful reviews and a series of screening processes to avoid costly excursions into the unknown which may simply represent an appealing or challenging hobby horse for the scientist. But scientists can counter that such efforts to plan things are incompatible with the serendipitous nature of discovery. The example of Fleming's discovery of penicillin has become a cliche, but a recent *Wall Street Journal* article[2] suggests that the point may nevertheless still be valid:

> James Schlatter was mixing amino acids, trying to come up with a test for an ulcer drug. The mix bubbled over and dripped down the outside of his flask.
>
> Later, the G. D. Searle & Co. researcher licked his finger to pick up a piece of paper and was startled. It tasted sweet. Curious, he retraced his steps, trying to figure where the sweetness had come from. Finally, he did: it was from the flask, flecked with the amino acids.
>
> That chance discovery on a cold winter day in 1965 has, nearly 20 years later, led to a red-hot product. It is the artificial sweetener aspartame, a simple combination of two amino acids. It can be found these days in soft drinks and chewing gum, puddings and powder-based beverages—and at Searle's bottom line.
>
> Less than three years after its debut, under the brand name Nutra-Sweet, aspartame will account for about half the company's $1.2 billion sales in 1984 and 70% of its profit. Those proportions keep growing, with sales expected to hit $1 billion by next year.

Scientists can also point to the inability to forecast future trends in the extraordinarily dynamic world of discovery. They could point with some amusement to the organizations that rejected Carlson's developments in what came to be called xerography (a process that was eventually supported by the smallish Haloid Company). Equally disillusioning to the proponents of careful plans and forecasts were those early estimates on computer usage which suggested that future markets might be limited in demand to 30 to 300 units throughout the entire United States.[3]

However, it would be a vast oversimplification to overstress this conflict between the needs and culture of pure science and the demands of pure business.[4] Scientists working in industry are neither naive nor simplistic. They recognize that continued funding for their more basic research is dependent upon the enthusiasm of senior management and that there must be some consistency between current business objectives and scientific directions.

Scientists as Entrepreneurs

Even more important and ignored by earlier studies of scientists in industry, many corporate scientists seek rewards beyond peer recognition. Particularly in companies such as "United" that stress new-venture management, ambitious scientists envision the monetary and ego rewards associated with riding a technical breakthrough until it becomes a successful free-standing commercial venture.

A good example of the urge to develop new products on the part of scientists is provided by Xerox's Palo Alto Research Center (PARC).[5] Throughout the 1970s, PARC was designated to do *solely* basic research for the corporation. While PARC was not supposed to do new-product development, this did in fact take place. For example, ALTO was a unique personal computer which was developed surreptitiously, and on behalf of which test marketing with the U.S. government and various universities was secretly attempted. ALTO was widely used and liked within the company, but because the product development unit was working on STAR—widely considered inferior—development of ALTO was not supported. Similarly, BRAVO, a unique text editing software product, was not supported by any product development unit.

We shall come back to the importance of linkages between R&D and marketing and product development in Chapters 3 and 4. Here, we want to emphasize only that it is less significant that there are opposed interests between scientists and business managers than that there are significant ongoing relationships. It is the function of the corporate R&D department to facilitate the interplay between scientific intuition and judgment and management strategy. Typically top management defines the fields of interest that will be explored by the department and thus provides basic guidance or limits. There is also ongoing interaction between the interest and results of R&D professionals and the business strategies of upper management.

19

Major Activities in the Corporate R&D Department

In the firm we studied most intensively, "United," the corporate R&D department had three budgets associated with three major categories of activities: exploratory research, research in support of the definition of new business opportunities, and research in support of already existing new ventures. This series of relations is illustrated in Figure 2-1.

In this chapter we shall examine the R&D department's decisions on funding for exploratory research. This represents one of the most critical decisions that shapes the relationship of the scientists to the organization.

In fact, the exploratory research programs are determined in relation to the domain of knowledge and competence that has been more or less explicitly defined by the firm as its own. This corresponds to the major areas of technology supporting the business activities of the operating divisions. The corporate R&D department serves to provide exploratory scientific expertise over and beyond what the divisional laboratories can supply. The corporate domain of knowledge, in turn (see Figure 2-1), is primarily the result of the historical resource commitments made over a period of time. There is a significant degree of inertia in exploratory research as a result of the long-term nature of research projects whose results can be assessed only after a number of years.

Another determinant of exploratory research programs is the new-business fields that the firm has recognized as having strategic importance for corporate development. As we shall see in Chapters 5 and 6, however, such fields tend to become concretely delineated only as the result of venture activities which then help to identify further specific needs for exploratory research. At the outset, new fields like "health" or "energy" are so general as to provide very little guidance for the scientists working in R&D departments.

While the R&D department is guided to some extent as to the type of research it will sponsor and encourage, it is thus important to recognize that this guidance is inevitably and desirably somewhat loose.[6] It is never obvious in research at a more basic level what the relationship will be between a given exploratory project and a given business objective. The boundaries between research subjects are ambiguous and in flux as new knowledge is created and new interrelations are uncovered. And, of course, researchers have their own in-

Figure 2–1

The Interrelation of the Major Innovative Activities Supported by the Corporate R&D Department

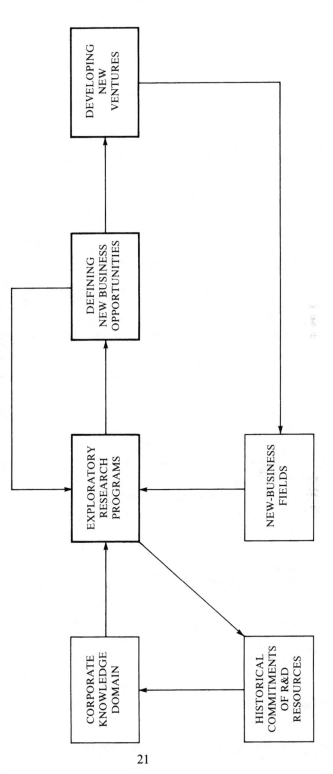

terests and fields of specialization. Inevitably they seek to bend and translate any research objective so that it encompasses what they wanted to accomplish in the first place.

Providing Managerial Direction for Exploratory Research

The director of the R&D department at United felt troubled about not having any good criteria for deciding how much of his discretionary budget should go into supporting the more amorphous fields in which the corporation had some interest and how much should go toward supporting more specific business objectives:

> My charter says that 15 percent of all funds should be spent on exploratory research. That sounds great, but actually it is the toughest thing in the world. It is difficult to decide how much resources to allocate to broad fields rather than to areas where there are clear business objectives.

In our study, we found that the more critical decisions are actually made by second-level supervisors, the R&D managers, each of whom is responsible for several "frontier" subject matter areas in science. It is the R&D managers' job to establish research programs for their staff—the group leaders and the "bench scientists." The R&D supervisors frequently spoke about the difficulty of deciding how much guidance to give, how tightly to control the research by initial definition and monitoring. For the most part they seemed to settle for establishing a very general direction and hoped to "keep their staff honest" by asking questions and demanding reviews. Some suggested it was like shooting in the dark; they knew what direction they wanted to go but couldn't see well enough to take aim.

One R&D manager expressed most succinctly what many others said more indirectly:

> You cannot write plans without the experts—and I am no longer an expert. The only thing I can do is to make a resource commitment and describe the scope within which we can then flesh out a program. So what I do is generate and set limits to research "envelopes," but I do not define specifically what goes into them. I can put limits on it, assign priorities, ask questions, go through project reviews, and give policy directions. Remember I have about 50 projects to oversee!

With the definition of the "envelope," a "narrowing down" process is set in motion involving the levels below the R&D manager, that is, the group leader and the bench researchers, and this leads to the establishment of specific objectives and action plans for each project. An R&D manager describes that process:

> The "envelope" is elastic in the beginning. In later phases it must be narrowed down. For instance, take the study of tree cell structure. We are interested in this general area for three reasons: (1) the possibility of growing trees in test tubes; (2) our interest in bioconversion and everything that pertains to cellulose; and (3) the possibility of producing chemicals through fermentation processes. Now if we want to pursue any of these, we need to know more.
>
> What we did has become part of the scientific establishment out in the field. Only then do you start to see the relevant specifics and begin to narrow down your objectives. For instance, pine trees go through a grass phase and only after a certain time do they start to grow as trees. Then we saw that it might be possible to make a tree that doesn't go through the grass phase. You cannot perceive something like that if you are not established in the area first. You need a road map.

Up from Below: Bench Scientist to Group Leader

The R&D manager and the corporate R&D director are involved in the establishment of the broad objectives, but the specific projects that will fill out these research programs are usually initiated by individual scientists. Their proposals, of course, must compete with each other and be assessed by the R&D managers on their relative merits.

R&D managers know that the corporate R&D Director at United is especially sensitive regarding two points. First, proposals should not overlap with ongoing R&D efforts in the operating divisions unless such divisions have specifically requested help. And second, projects should be avoided that require adding new personnel who would be redundant if the project were to turn out not to be successful. In a sense the first constraint encourages more departures from established research domains, while the second constraint acts in a more conservative direction and tends to limit departures into new research areas. Existing technical considerations impose some limits on the type and scale of projects that can be considered.

R&D managers act as idea brokers. When effective, they maintain reasonably frequent contacts with upper management to know what areas are acceptable and what "tailoring" may be necessary to get a scientist's research interests under the wire. This enables them to guide research ideas that have been initiated by scientists and channeled through the group leaders.

R&D managers must also learn to persevere. Unlike nonmanagers who may believe naively that a good idea should sell itself, R&D managers know they must be willing to bring the same proposal up several times before it may get approval for funding or before it should be abandoned.

R&D managers must sell their total program to the director of corporate R&D, and the better salespeople they are the more of the laboratory's total budget they will likely command. Here is how one successful R&D manager views the process.

> First I must be convinced or I can't sell the project. I decide after comparing various projects with each other which ones to support and seek authorizations for. If it is a new area for us, the director may agree but he is likely to say in 1 year I want to review the results. If they are good, the second year will be quite easy.
>
> Overall it looks as though if one keeps things the same from one accounting period to the next it is much easier. If you want to take something away or put something new in, that is when the controversy can begin.

Thus it appears that there is less experimentation in the formal authorization process than one would expect in a basic research environment. After all, it is difficult to know whether a project will be worthwhile without some experimentation. However, as we shall see, this conservative bias toward continuity is corrected for by allowing "unauthorized" research.

Group Leaders

These are the people who are most "in the middle" from the point of view of management and the scientists. Managers above this level can afford to be somewhat obsolete, that is, to be truly managers, not scientists. But group leaders need broad nets of contact and sources of information to assess what is state-of-the-art, what is new and promising, and to evaluate what is demanded of them by scientists seeking research budgets for new projects. This balance between participating in research and managing it was expressed by one quite candid group leader:

> All of us start out as specialists. I think of myself as having been hopefully a world expert in some narrow area at one time. But as you go up (in the hierarchy) you must deal with a greater diversity. My problem is that I cannot be an expert any longer in everything I deal with; so I must start relying on other people. Also, it's an ego thing. You want to be a professional scientist. But just as important, it helps to be one, because you can get lots of information if you are respected in the scientific community. I must be able to stay part of this network of unpublished information.

It is the group leaders who feel most painfully the struggle between relevance of a specific research area to the corporation and the needs of "science," at least science as perceived by their scientist colleagues/subordinates in the department.

Bench Scientists

While we have sought to describe the process of project authorization as a working through of legitimately differing viewpoints, bench researchers are frequently derisive of the efforts of upper-level technical managers to make proposals. They sense what the managers themselves fear; namely, that one quickly becomes technically obsolete. As on scientist said with some scorn:

> Sure, there are times when research ideas come down from above. An R&D manager may read something in *Scientific American*, and that gets him interested in a topic. Of course, by the time it appears there, it's already out of vogue in the *real* scientific world.

Unfortunately, to the researchers, upper levels of management are often perceived as capricious rather than thoughtful. The definitions of the "envelopes" and the "narrowing down" process seem ad hoc, "knee jerk" reactions to outside information sources of questionable quality: semipopular science journals, consultants, and so forth. In the words of one young bench researcher:

> We will find something out in the lab, and we will tell management. They will talk to consultants, friends; even their spouses will have an in-

put too. All these elements get blended and lead them to react to the idea. Usually that means a narrowing down; a cycle has been started.

After we have brought up something, they will forget about it until they are confronted with the same thing in the outside world. Then they come back; management now thinks that they have originated the idea! Wall Street will come up with something, and that becomes "the" thing. The presidents of our competitors will chat about it. That is how the world works.

The higher you go up in the management hierarchy, the narrower the objectives get defined interpreted. Ultimately, the group leader "dictates" and "directs" research. If this narrowing down process happens to you a number of times, then you start to go as the book says.

This scientist, along with others, is observing a central problem in the relationship of managers and technically trained personnel. Managers appear to oscillate between excessively broad and restrictively narrow objectives. From a scientist's point of view, both stem from a failure to understand what is knowledge or an inability to deal with the conceptual complexity of innovations.

Thus managers may say, for example, "We ought to be utilizing lasers in some new products." Scientists would say that is too broad to be a meaningful direction. Equally discouraging is the tendency of senior management to get very narrow and specific by announcing, "We should be moving into cutting tools."

The scientist wants to look at fundamental natural processes. Ideally the scientist's norms direct work toward projects involving *narrow*—that is, highly specific—experiments. However, these narrow experiments, if successful, will have very *broad* implications. Thus the scientists are scornful of the nonscientists' misplaced concreteness or their naivete about a new stream of research. They argue that truly innovative products only grow out of their kind of direction, that is, well-conceived experimentation, not vague notions of new frontiers to conquer.

Given reasonable self-confidence about their abilities and the wisdom of their scientific methods, most researchers do not get "turned off" by the naivete of management. Instead they bide their time and find ways to keep their specific ideas alive. As one researcher put it:

For me "dreaming" is important. You "moonlight"; you don't quit; you keep developing the story, but do not push at the wrong time. I do my own thing, but put it in a "compiler" to translate it into management's language.

The Functions of "Bootleg" Research

One phenomenon that characterizes all R&D environments is the existence of "bootleg" or "nonprogrammed" research: projects that are carried out by researchers but that are "informal" insofar as they are not formally authorized in the department's action plans and resource allocations. As Donald Hammond, Director of Hewlett-Packard's physical electronics laboratory, put it, "We encourage our people to take about 10% of their time for under-the-bench projects or their own pet projects."[7]

One explanation for these "bootleg" research programs is that ideas sometimes come up in the intervals between the times when resource commitments are made, and in order not to lose them they are funded informally for the time being. As one R&D manager put it, "I always keep some reserve money to allow people to start something in the middle of the budgetary year." Another reason is that invention is abundant and unpredictable, and that researchers need an outlet for their creative energies; bootleg projects are a natural way to absorb this. From our research, however, a third and maybe the most important but least obvious explanation emerges. Bootleg projects are actually encouraged to some extent by R&D managers because they can serve as "demonstration projects." Aware of their limited capacity to judge the real merits of the projects defined by their group leaders, R&D managers use the tactic of encouraging the group leaders to substantiate their claims with such demonstration projects. In the words of another R&D manager:

> The group leaders will say the same thing about me as what I say about the business people: they will say that I always tell them "it's perfectly good idea, but we need our money for other things." I encourage them to do "bootleg research"; to come back when they have results.

R&D managers encourage this practice, because the results of it—the demonstration project—allow them to bridge the discrepancy between their actual involvement in the research proposal and their authority to fund them. Such projects also allow the laboratory to treat the more reasonable and safe projects in one way (formal funding) and the more risky ones in another (informal funding).

In effect, lower-level scientists engage in "strategic initiatives." However, upper management structures the "arenas" within which these initiatives compete for support from the organization. This approach should assure a "fit" between the survivors and the "enveloped" objectives. But it is worth noting that the "envelope" is not at all rigid, as we have seen, and it becomes further shaped by these demonstration projects.

From Exploratory Research to
the Definition of New Business Opportunities

Exploratory research starts with the definition of "envelopes" by the R&D manager level. These envelopes set the boundaries and parameters within which a "narrowing down" process takes place which results in the definition of specific objectives and programs by the group leader level. Parallel with these formal efforts, a number of informal bootleg research projects are initiated by individual researchers and group leaders and "condoned" by the R&D managers. Out

Figure 2–2
The Intervening Processes Between Exploratory Research
and the Definition of New Business Opportunities

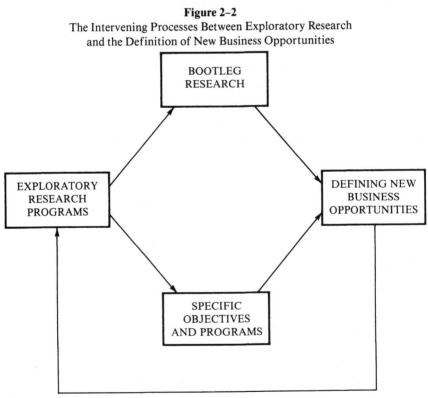

of these interaction processes result the ideas for new technologies, products, and systems that are necessary for the definition of new business opportunities. The latter, if successful, will lead to a redefinition of the "envelopes" and to additional specific, now-formalized, objectives. These relationships are depicted in Figure 2-2.

The definition process of a new business comprises, in actuality, two stages: a *conceptualization* stage and a *pre-venture* stage. The conceptualization stage involves activities that lead to the identification of a new business opportunity involving preliminary technical and market research. The pre-venture stage involves the formation of a team of R&D and business people around preliminary business objectives and plans, and leads to the first efforts to commercialize a new product, process, or system. These stages will be discussed in detail in Chapters 2 through 4.

From Definition to Development of a New Business

The actual development process of a new business also comprises two stages: an *entrepreneurial* stage and an *organizational* stage. The entrepreneurial stage involves the transfer of an embryonic business with autonomous venture status to the new-business development department in the new-venture division. It leads to the transformation of the embryonic business into a viable "one-product type" business under the impulse of an entrepreneurial venture manager. The organizational stage involves the transformation of the one-product busi-

Figure 2–3
Stages in ICV Development

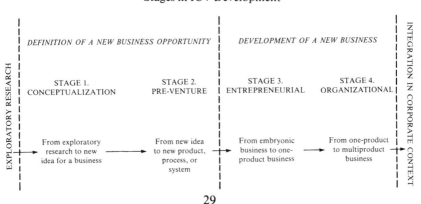

29

ness into a complex "multiproduct" business, ready to be integrated as a full-fledged member of the corporation's operating system. These stages are discussed in detail in Chapters 6 and 7.

The four stages involved in defining and developing a new business are represented in Figure 2-3.

CHAPTER 3

Transforming Invention into Innovation

The Conceptualization Stage

Understandably we think of strategy formulation as top management work. Most employees, even quite high-level managerial employees, take the goals of the business as a given. But in the high-technology world, strategy often revolves around the innovation activities of relatively low-level technical and business people. To be sure, their decisions will require ratification by top management. Nevertheless, as noted in Chapter 2, the reality is that those closer to the emerging technology will seek to define the business opportunity.

Creating a new business opportunity, however, goes beyond "invention." "Innovation" involves welding marketplace opportunities with inventive technology and new technical knowledge. This requires substantial skill and it is by no means a simple decision-making process. For instance, a new plastic could or might be translated into any number of new products. Since there are still very many implementation unknowns as to how a laboratory breakthrough can be more completely understood, modified, and controlled—and eventually mass-produced economically—selecting the commercial applications of any new discovery is highly problematic. Marketing new products resulting from technological breakthroughs is equally problematic. Depending on future technological developments, which are still unknown, one or more markets *may* be visible. But these markets can also be elusive, particularly when one is dealing with products that users have not previously experienced.

To lead to the development of a potentially successful new business, the marketing strategy must also take into account corporate interests. Further investment in business development will be forthcoming only if the definitions of the product and market are in a field that the company considers consistent with its legitimate domain, present and future. In Chapters 5 and 6 we shall see that the process whereby the link between a new business and the corporate context becomes established involves complex strategic activities on the part of various levels of management, but at this point it suffices to observe that project initiators must (and do) attempt to anticipate whether a new development *could possibly* be acceptable given the "fabric" of the corporation. The notion of the "fabric" of the corporation is inherently vague, never quite completely delineated; it is always in the process of being stretched as a result of the strategic initiations that people at the operational level are attempting to engage in.

Thus three elements must be brought together by R&D managers and/or new-venture managers in their efforts at strategy formulation: (1) technical competency, (2) market need, and (3) corporate interest. How is this done? Whose job should it be? How can management evaluate whether it is being done effectively? Does a new venture fail because some failure is inevitable with all the unknowns present when the strategy must be formulated, or because the managerial patterns and practices in making the decision were faulty? To answer these questions one needs to know something about the process by which these decisions are made. And by process we mean how individual managers and scientists link up those three elements.

The history of corporate innovation is replete with the development of exciting new technical breakthroughs that did not lead to viable products. And, in fact, there is no reason to believe that most new knowledge has any immediate application. Basic researchers have warned that this is true, but there is the natural temptation to believe that new laboratory phenomena *must* have commercial implications and, more naively, that the more interesting the breakthrough the greater is its commercial value.

In contrast, there are always efforts to define a market need and seek to "invent-to-order" a product for that need. The government occasionally even publishes lists of the most-wanted inventions, but such presumed market inducements, in themselves, don't seem to produce relevant new technologies.

Conceptualization of New Business Opportunities

The evolution of the method of managing this process at United appears to be similar to that which has taken place in many corporate R&D functions. Initially, when it was recognized that some welding of specializations was necessary, it was hoped that R&D could add market specialists on an ad hoc basis—as advisors or consultants when necessary. Gradually, as recognition of the importance of the marketing side grew, a permanent, formalized "business research function" was added to the R&D function to help shape new ventures and increase the odds that new products would be successfully commercialized.

Some senior managers expected that the market specialists would gradually take the lead in strategy formulation by seeking to define research objectives. Others assumed the scientists and business researchers would work together.

The managerial initiatives associated with R&D at this exploratory stage can be defined in three alternative patterns:

1. Marketing-oriented managers can direct scientists into what appear to be exciting markets with assured high demand. (This is often called, in fact, "demand pull.") Here innovation, the need, is father to (or mother to) the new "invention."

2. Scientists, attuned to the realities of the corporation's interests, look for new technologies and scientific breakthroughs with good commercialization potential. (This is called "technology push.")

3. Marketing and scientific specialists work together, bringing their own skills to a joint endeavor to develop new technology with sound market possibilities.

Any of these three patterns is a good theoretical possibility, but only one predominated at United.

33

The Predominance of "Technology Push"

At United, it was clear that most new-product efforts got their initial definition on the basis of "technology push."[1] In part, this reflected the need for highly sophisticated knowledge about science and technology, about what is feasible and what isn't, about what the odds are that something can be accomplished, and about what the resulting new product is likely to have in the way of basic characteristics. While it sounds feasible that dialogues should occur between business and science spokespeople, they may be less constructive at this very early stage than they obviously are at a somewhat later stage of the development process. An example may show why the "partnership" arrangement is not as productive as would be presumed:

> The laboratory has pioneered in developing a new high-strength material. Given its characteristics market research said the new material's ideal application was vehicle parts, because of its strength-to-weight ratio. Furthermore, given their knowledge of motor vehicle manufacturers, market research proposed one or two vehicle parts that would represent an ideal market to penetrate. Unfortunately these specific uses would require further technological breakthroughs that would be incredibly difficult to guarantee. In fact, the laboratory scientists estimated that there might be only a handful of researchers in the world who could make the needed technological advances. The market researchers never could appreciate why it was so difficult to go from the basic discovery to the ultimate commercial application they had envisioned.

There will be dozens if not hundreds of such trade-offs among cost, feasibility, and application that require a great deal of technical knowledge and experience. In addition, United placed great emphasis on what it called attaining a "sustainable position." It sought to have a "technological lock" on any new product. While it is questionable that patents represent an absolute barrier to competition, United sought to develop unique, patentable technologies.

It is not surprising then that the major trade-offs and early decisions at United were made inside the head of a single technically trained person. Usually this individual would be a technologist who wanted to accomplish an impressive business goal such as developing a product that would have enormous economic implications. These scientist-entrepreneurs took it upon themselves to link up their conception of what ideas are marketable with new technological discoveries coming both from within and outside of their own laboratory.

They often traveled around the world gleaning information on potentially marketable scientific breakthroughs. Their goal was to tie together emerging knowledge with a challenging technical issue or problem.

Here is a typical example of how an R&D scientist develops interests and seeks to develop projects that will lead to new products.

Opportunities, in my view, come up as technical problems. As a result of certain interest trends in my division, I had gotten interested in molecules that had been heated up to high temperatures. Because the technical problems usually turn out to be quite different than they are initially defined, I come to see much more fundamental questions . . . which is what led me to engage in research at the frontiers of organic chemistry.

In the field at the time there was one particular technical problem that interested me . . . a very difficult to control transformation process. There was a researcher in France who had learned how to exercise fine control. I thought that if I could really learn how the process works, how to control it, it would surely have some real business applications.

Essentially these scientists—through reading and contacts in the field—identify exciting frontier areas in their respective fields that appear to have some conceivable relationship to what have been defined as corporate interests. They also of course seek to link up new developments that have been created in other parts of their corporate R&D world, that is, the R&D sectors of the operating divisions.

Ten years ago I and others became aware of the fact that our corporation was developing substantial new technology in one aspect of the electronic controls field. This led to a separate division being created, and I began working on controls as applied to the health field, but with the recession it became difficult to get a heavy R&D commitment to that area. Therefore I was pleased when I got shifted to the corporate R&D labs which had a health-related technology program. There we looked for health applications of the kind of technology we were developing that would be a major market.

About this time I visited another lab of the corporation and I met a scientist there who had developed a unique but related technology that could be developed, I felt, into a product that would be far superior to anything in the field.

Broadly speaking, the experienced technologist looks for ideas and scientific breakthroughs that might provide new-product leverage. Often this means linking up work being done in the corporate

35

R&D laboratory with data being generated in some other organization. Through personal contacts, reading, and attending meetings the scientist does what management personnel call "environmental scanning," that is, seeking to see some synthesis or synergy between ideas and fields of knowledge that competitors may have missed.

> We were pursuing a field of inquiry relating to some development going on in one of the operating divisions and I thought I should try to put the two together. When I began working with them, I gained access to some complementary research in a government laboratory on the West Coast that they had been collaborating with. I was now getting close to something that might have some real commercial possibilities.

This is what management should expect of its R&D personnel: the ability not only to conduct relevant research but to monitor and link up with other relevant work wherever it may be going on, and to see some overall pattern or implication in these diverse streams.

Figure 3–1 represents a model embodying the typical sequence of "linkages" followed in the evolution of a technology-driven exploratory strategy.

Such linkages can fail, of course, even when technical personnel find interesting problems and possible solutions but when their ideas

Figure 3–1
The Flow of Activities in the "Technology Push" Model

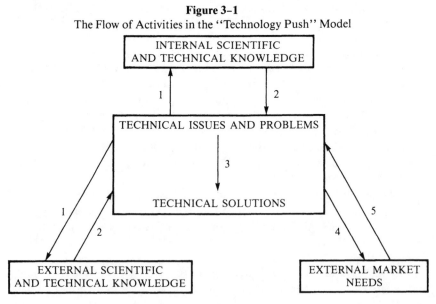

do not match corporate interests and cannot be woven into the corporate "fabric":

> In another case, I was interested in high-temperature materials and that got me into boron chemistry. This was also the result of my interacting with colleagues in academia. I began to get interested in making these boron-based materials less expensively, but these materials were outside of the corporation's experience. There was some interest in the Defense Department and we came very close to proving its business importance, but the linking-up failed; we couldn't get corporate management interested; it was out of their realm.

Thus, the technologist still faces the problem of gaining financial support for his conception. This is the classic chicken-and-egg problem. It is difficult to "prove" the usefulness of this new approach without adequate funding. But adequate funding usually depends upon being able to show very good data and results, which in turn require that funding. The "bootleg research" we described in Chapter 2 is one first step around this vicious circle.

At times changing circumstances convert a skimpily supported effort to an all-out campaign. The energy crisis of a couple of years ago was one of the most profound stimulants.

> We had been working on new types of insulation for years but when the energy crisis occurred everyone realized that we might have a number of immediate applications. I knew of our experience and work in this area and I formulated a proposal for a 2- to 5-year effort for our top management review committee. As an additional impetus I was able to show that moving on this front would help us move in a direction that had often been talked about in the corporation—getting out of becoming a basic supplier of commodity-type materials into higher-margined finished products.

Problems with "Technology Push"

But such enthusiasm and confidence cannot compensate for some defects inherent in an overemphasis on "technology push." Perhaps the most obvious is that a scientist-entrepreneur's orientation toward understanding some basic phenomenon and solving a tough technological problem will tend to encourage market applications that are the most easily researched and evaluated.

In one of our cases, a new material being developed was applied to a rather easily fabricated consumer product. In fact, as a marketing person added later to the project later discovered, the real potential application was in a very different class of product.

A more serious pitfall of technology-driven projects is that they are more likely to get locked into a particular technical solution.

The company developed an interest in a high-technology area in the biological field. The efforts were directed by a Ph.D. who some years before had developed an innovative method of separating materials at the molecular level. Such separation was an important step in producing certain new products in which we became interested. But, as we later realized, Dr. X's technique, as interesting as it was, wasn't the best way of making the transition to large-scale manufacture. But as long as Dr. X was in charge, alternative methods would not be explored.

Of course, one could argue—with some justification—that if Dr. X hadn't helped make the initial technological breakthrough the company might not have become interested in this particular biological field. However, at the early conceptual stage it is important to keep options open. A specific technological innovation may have hidden defects or may turn out to be less useful than predicted for the class of end products that are most marketable. As long as the key decisions are being made primarily by the "father of the invention" it is possible that ends will be confused with means. Here is another example:

Another researcher developed a new type of seed tape which was designed for large-scale agricultural use. Further exploration disclosed that such a process would be useful primarily in greenhouses growing seedlings, not in open fields. The real market opportunity was seen now as producing transplants rather than simply a new seed carrier (i.e., the tape).

A related pitfall of the "technology push" mode is that there is a tendency to address the needs of atypical users and to invoke their acceptance of the new product, process, or system as evidence for the existence of a new business "opportunity." The scientist-entrepreneur has a knack for coming up with convincing evidence to demonstrate the "interest" of prospective users. As one scientist–turned–business manager put it, "If you address yourself to the 'right' people in any market, you will hear them say: 'Wow! This is what we have been waiting for.'"[2] This process of selectively addressing atypical potential customers is especially dangerous if the technical linking-up process has not been adequately performed to begin with. Early success with an inadequate technical system used by an atypical customer can lead to the erroneous projection of market potential.

While we have said that successful technologists-entrepreneurs do concern themselves with the user marketplace (and the corporate marketplace for ideas), they are limited in the sophistication with which they can do this. Those with business training and experience, particularly in analyzing and estimating markets, can make an important contribution. In fact, it is often felt that such people should take the initiative in defining a new-product strategy.

"Need Pull" Dominance

Experienced management consultants like McKinsey believe that R&D can be targeted—in advance—by specific market goals:

> An experienced photochemist, Dr. Hans Schleussner, owner-manager of a medium-sized West German pharmaceutical company, put together a three-person team to work on a project to develop blood substitutes. It took them just 2½ years to find a plasma substitute, which led to the establishment of a new business for Schleussner, revived the entire market for gelatine preparations, and left the large pharmaceutical companies to catch up, at great expense, over the next 3 to 4 years.[3]

From a personnel point of view, a major distinction of "need pull" from "technology push" is a division of labor. In the "need pull" model, the definition and exploration of markets are usually handled by a business/marketing-trained specialist. This individual's identification of a high-potential market initiates a search process for inside- or outside-the-firm technical knowledge that might be used to develop an innovative product to enter that market.

The actual sequence we observed is depicted in Figure 3–2.

Experienced new-venture managers recognize that market needs have to be defined in terms that avoid the following two extremes: superficial broad generalizations (e.g., "materials for home building") or very narrow applications with limited potential (e.g., "cabinet hinge material"). To bridge these extremes, a narrowing or focusing

39

Figure 3–2
The Flow of Activities in the "Need Pull" Model

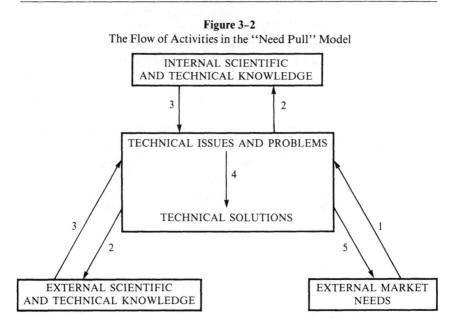

process takes place. But this too has its own problems. In particular, the process breeds confusion for the R&D people, who must keep redesigning their technology to fit a perpetually moving target. Or, immediate market demands may override a consideration of more fundamental long-range trends. For instance, in the early 1970s a company called "Accuracy" acquiesced to its salespeople's demand for a process control system that would use both digital and analog computers, ignoring the trend that would make analog computers obsolete.[4]

Also, too many market-oriented compromises can destroy a basically sound innovative idea. John Newhouse[5] tells the story of an aeronautical engineer with American Airlines who foresaw the need for smaller jets. He wanted to develop a two-engine, relatively lightweight plane seating 150 passengers, which would fill the airline's need for a practical, economical plane to fly out of LaGuardia to the Midwest. As McDonnell-Douglas and Lockheed explored other customer requirements, they saw that there was a need for more range and climbing ability—with the resulting addition of more weight. A plane with more weight required a third engine; this led to the development of the DC-10 and the L-1011, two planes with essentially the same design. The market for a smaller plane was completely missed and was eventually filled first by a European manufacturer with the A-300B aircraft (Airbus Industrie).

Following the same line of thought, users or customers often do not have a clear idea of their own needs with respect to a truly new product, and "conventional wisdom" about customers or users can kill a potentially successful innovation. *The New York Times* recently told about a GE engineer who invented the cassette in 1952, "But he left his important invention to gather dust after a GE executive told him, 'There is no future in tape'."

When the sought-for innovation is going to be an element in a larger system manufactured by an outside user, the market research problems can be most complex and there will be great leeway for error.

> We were designing a key component for aircraft using our new Z material. The more we looked the more we realized how much we needed to understand the interaction of almost all of the components and particularly the effect of stressful usage and what future maintenance people will want and how they will operate. Simply designing a first-rate component was a long way from the solution.
>
> So you learn that you cannot seek to develop a new part in isolation; you need to analyze all the stresses in the system as they impact the part and then translate these into requirements of your new high-strength material and see how you can design it to minimize the more costly elements.

If one of the risks of "technology push" is developing a solution for which there turns out to be no problem, the "need pull" approach faces the possibly greater risk of not being able to generate the required technology to solve an existing problem either in-house or through acquisition. Said one participant from the business side:

> Many applications have started with a given technology. The problem is then to see how you build a business with that technology, how to acquire a proprietary position and capitalize on it. Our "plating" business actually started with a focus on the larger market and the identification of opportunities, and we then tried to develop the technology. It's a more risky approach. You might do a lot of fine work but never reach your goals. One alternative way is to use an acquisition strategy. But that is very risky too. Even if you buy ten companies, there can still be an eleventh one that has the real key to the technology.

Perhaps the most serious shortcoming of "need pull" is the absence of a "true believer." For the new-business market analyst, this potential product is but one of a number that may be in the process of being researched. There is no assurance that even "if it flies" it will be backed up by the new-business marketing specialist. Not only is future promise lacking as an additional motivation, but there is no past commitment. After all, the idea is usually not the brainchild of the analyst who has been assigned to investigate its commercial potential.

In contrast, the technical person who becomes a "product champion" (see Chapter 5 for a discussion of this role) has a sense of being identified with an idea or a discovery or at least with a systematic line of research reflecting his or her own competencies and interest. Even more importantly, in United as in many corporate R&D laboratories, a successful definition of a new-product venture can bring with it the possibility of major advancement. It can become a vehicle for increased visibility, for becoming a new-venture manager and even the head of a major new business. And as we have noted before, some scientists in corporate laboratories find these highly appealing prospects; they really do want to jump from pure research to pure management.

Projects at this exploratory stage meet lots of resistance in the laboratory, the marketplace, and the corporate budget process. To some extent their viability depends upon gaining momentum—giving key managers the sense that this project has favorable odds and is moving forward. Hence, a degree of initial success is necessary to attract interest and support.

The Double Linking Required

We have been describing the technical-linking and need-linking processes. Both are necessary for successful innovation.

Technical linking requires someone who can combine a promising technical problem (e.g., increasing the durability of a fiber)—one that is recognized as falling within the broad boundaries of the corporation's domains of interest—with external and/or internal scientific knowledge. The researcher-conceptualizer views the *solution* of this technical problem as both feasible and relevant. It is by means of the technical sophistication possessed by the researcher-conceptualizer that this individual can recognize that this is a sensible, realistic problem to be working on at this time. The process of technical linking leads to the realization that working on a particular problem represents taking a "logical" step forward, one that may lead to a possible technological breakthrough with profitable consequences for the corporation.

The other linking-up that must be undertaken at the same time relates to needs. It represents the ability to perceive interrelationships between these existing or potential technical breakthroughs in the laboratory and actual or potential market demand. Essentially this linking asserts that if X can be accomplished, and routinized—commercialized within a suitable price range—then there will be a market of this size.

"Technology Push" and "Need Pull" Models Compared

Below we have summarized the deficiencies and shortcomings of the two approaches to strategy formulation at the exploratory stage:

"TECHNOLOGY PUSH"	"NEED PULL"
• Start with what easily can be researched and evaluated	• Look at needs that are easily identified but with minor potential
• Address the needs of the atypical user	• Continue to change the definition of the "opportunity"; "miss the opportunity"
• Get locked into one technical solution	• Lack a "champion" or "true believer"

Corporate Interests

New-venture projects of the nature described here typically fall outside of the current strategy of the firm. To be sure, as we described earlier, top management seeks to define the industries and business that it would find appealing. To the extent that these go beyond the interests of the operating divisions, however, they are so broadly defined, for example, "health," "food," or "energy," as to be virtually useless as a guide for concrete action. In fact, what we found was the emergence of new fields out of small areas of commercial activity related to specific projects originating at the operational level. This was most clear from the analysis of the written documents at United. In 1975, the corporate long-range plan for the new-venture division read:

> Instead of dealing with an ever-growing number of separate arenas, attention should be focused on a critical few major fields, within each of which arenas may be expanded, grouped together, or added.

Yet no matter who seeks to be the proponent of a new venture and argue its viability, ultimately it must be accepted by higher management. Proponents of new ventures, therefore, needed to understand what kind of project would be acceptable to top management. Even more important, it seemed, was their capability to stay away from projects that would be perceived by top management as *not* consistent with the external image of the firm, or that might lead to dangerous potential legal liabilities. In the health field, for instance, people knew that top management was concerned about entering therapeutic rather than diagnostic segments.

Thus, the three elements must be considered together in order to define a viable new business opportunity (Table 3-1).

It was, then, perhaps not surprisingly, a group leader who usually turned out to be the driving force in the definition of a new business opportunity. Such people have enough contact with the substantive research process to understand and direct the technical linking process, sufficient contact with the business side to think in terms of market needs, and the organizational experience required to under-

Table 3-1
Three Elements Requiring Linkage

1 Relevant "Problems"	2 Technology Sources	3 Market Demand
As defined by top management's professed "interests"	Researcher's personal interests	Marketer's personal search
Problems of operating divisions	Existing corporate expertise	Areas of customer dissatisfaction
New opportunities created by external events	New technological developments	Potential for new need satisfaction

stand how new technological breakthroughs could be "woven into the fabric" of the firm.

Effective Conceptualization

Such successful managers are synthesizers, able to put together and link ongoing technical streams with existing corporate commitments and directions and then to relate these to market needs. Success is dependent on the simultaneous, almost serendipitous occurrence of a number of mutually compatible requirements and resources. The link to the market is frequently neglected: the explicit requirements of customers, competitive pressures, size and durability of the demand, and opportunities for synergies and economies of scale.

A remarkable example of the importance of having people who can perform the *double* linking process is provided by the story of Steve Jobs of Apple Computer visiting Xerox's Palo Alto Research Center:

> In December 1979, Steve Jobs, then Apple's vice-chairman, visited PARC with some colleagues to poke around. They saw "smalltalk," a set of programming tools. "Their eyes bugged out," recalls Lawrence Tesler who helped develop "smalltalk." "They understood its significance better than anyone else who had visited." Seven months later, Jobs hired Tesler, having decided to use many "smalltalk" features in the Lisa.[7]

Here is a carefully conceptualized strategy that meets our criteria:

> United's focus should be on certain special organic acids that have a very complex molecular structure, are difficult to synthesize and where various governmental and market forces assure a premium price for the output of the type of processing we will be doing and where a number of related products can be developed that will allow us to build an economical multipurpose facility.

A small number of development managers have the skill and insight to combine the technological and market emphases at this very early stage of the cycle. The example below represents one of the most successful innovations we followed:

> I had worked in the computer field and knew the importance of matching a technology with the market configuration. When I took on the Z project I soon learned that the technology we were utilizing had also been adopted by another company seeking to enter this same market.

My company had gotten very interested in a novel idea being developed by one of the scientists in one of our satellite laboratories. After some discussion it was clear that this could be directly applied to the development of a new line of diagnostic instruments that would have major advantages over what is now being produced. The scientist, however, was very rigid: the equipment had to follow his original conceptions and breakthroughs.

As Z project manager I insisted on doing market research, and from that learned of customer needs that would not be satisfied by the original conception. We also learned that there was a substantial market to be tapped having to do with the reagents needed to operate the equipment. So we ended up with a radical departure, using only the nucleus of the scientist's physical concepts. We added a very different data "reader," a minicomputer, and so forth.

Even when the two processes—technology and market linkages—are combined there is no guarantee of success. The following case is typical of how a company develops interests in funding a new area of development and some of the ensuing problems:

The corporation recognized there might be some commercial potential in its filtration expertise. I wrote a position paper on the state of the art in this field and where we stood. It was decided we should do further work in the area. In the course of our R&D work we developed a unique product that seemed to have applications to the pollution problems of one particular major industry. We even were able to develop a test installation.

I now had proof of a well-operating installation, so I asked myself how many of these installations could be needed in the market: ten thousand or so? Now I had to make a judgment as to how many of these potential customers were likely to go our way. To do so, you must know the alternatives for these customers; you must talk to the pollution control people. Then you must put together these facts, and on this basis—what people have told you—you make your projections.

Eventually, a market study was done that said that there was not going to be a big enough market for a gas separation method but there was a hint in the report—and it was really just a hint—that there just might be an opportunity for liquid filtering. So we got into it and soon found out that the product we had was not adequate!

A Classification Scheme

As we review the examples above, it seems relatively easy to allot them to one of the cells in the matrix shown in Figure 3–3. While we

46

Figure 3–3
Emphasis on "Technical" and "Need Linking"

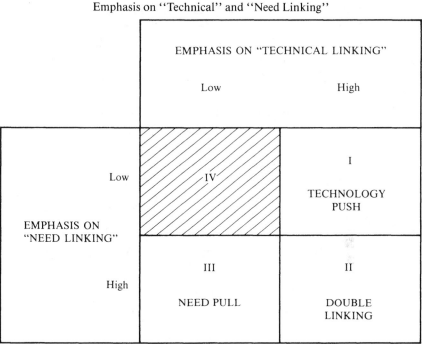

would be hard-pressed to provide statistical proof, the most successful ventures appeared to be those in quadrant II (double linking).

Most new ventures in R&D-oriented corporations appear to be in the domain of technology. The technology managers concentrate on linking up inside and outside knowledge in the development of prototype solutions (product, process, or system) that will also be consistent with some market or need analysis. As that is defined and there is some proof of technical feasibility, the first business plans are conceptualized.

Innovation Traps

While at times there is extraordinarily good fortune and the original conceptualization turns out to be the best, more realistically, better definitions are made when there is flexibility and modification. Innovative technology stimulates the search for commercial applications. Efforts to explore potential business applications reveal defects in the original technological conception leading to the search

47

for modified or different technological approaches. For such flexibility to be present during conceptualization it is important that scientists maintain their perspective. Being overly committed or identified with a given "solution" can injure the scientist's ability to realistically appraise technological breakthroughs in the light of market considerations. Such scientists observably err by defining the problems with which they are coping in such narrow terms that only one solution, namely "their" solution, will do.

Management can evaluate the quality of their developmental personnel by observing which individuals have the flexibility to modify or even drop technical solutions in the light of new data, new constraints, or need-derived problems. Such researchers may begin a project with great enthusiasm for a specific breakthrough they have made or have become familiar with, but as their research progresses they are able to spot the flaws in this particular technology and seek alternatives. Often the alternatives can turn out to be even more worthwhile than the original breakthrough.

> During the early days of the National Aeronautics and Space Administration (NASA) science program it was decided to orbit a telescope, and the chief scientist evolved a design that included a very costly lens that could be produced only in one foreign laboratory. Both the cost and the delay inherent in procuring that particular lens motivated the person to link the chief scientist with the engineers who would actually be responsible for the satellite, and the need for that particular lens was challenged. The proponent of the lens insisted that it was the only one that would provide the resolution power that designated use demanded. When he was told that it could not be procured because the whole program would suffer costly delays, he was able to modify another lens that had been developed in the United States. The cost was a fraction of the original estimate of the foreign lens and the new lens proved even more powerful than the original specifications demanded.[8]

There can also be too much flexibility. On the market side this can reflect itself in unrealistic demands for invention or technical solutions because "this is what the market demands." Sometimes this leads to expectations and even promises to management that can't be delivered. Those in charge of marketing may be unresponsive to what scientists say is feasible or deliverable. In this case the wish is not father to the child, so to speak.

There may also be too much flexibility on the technical side when, for instance, scientists jump in too quickly to fill a niche that has been defined by top management or the environment as timely and obviously supportable. When it is too easy to get funding and encouragement, scientists may fail to "do their homework" and may rush to implement a new technology that has not been worked through and questioned adequately, or seek to find an "all-purpose" solution to a broad and complex problem like the energy crisis.

Finally, a trap can exist at this conceptualization stage when the market success of the innovation is too dependent on a potentially variable environmental component of the market. United got trapped into developing costly or cumbersome pollution control systems that could only be viable with a strict level of governmental enforcement of certain regulations. Similar mistakes can be made when it is assumed in a cavalier fashion that a given resource that is now in short supply will always be in short supply or, alternatively, that a surplus of a given resource will exist forever.

CHAPTER 4

Conceiving New
Business Opportunities
The Interface Between
Business and R&D People

A new business opportunity, an innovation, requires a merging of an exploratory research breakthrough with an existing or potential market. At times companies have sought to produce innovations sequentially. The laboratory completes a technological development and its work is transferred to a more business-oriented exploration of the market potential. However, such a sequence ignores the reality of most new-product development. Rarely do the original scientific "invention" and the exploratory research on the market flow smoothly to a salable product. Both the conception of the technology and the definition of the market are usually in a state of flux. Each influences the other: what is feasible influences what can be sold and what is required by the customer helps shape what the laboratory seeks to develop.

Thus large corporations seek to integrate the efforts of scientists and business managers with a marketing bent in an organizational setting devoted to giving birth to new business opportunities. They seek a setting in which technological and market ideas can be simultaneously, rather than sequentially, explored—at least that is the ideal case.

While this cooperation must persist over a long period of time throughout the development cycle, the most critical phase is in the beginning. At this point there are the most options. However, it is difficult to maintain equality of input from the business and technical divisions. It is not hard to understand why. The orientation of these two sets of professionals is so very different that easy and balanced give-and-take is rare, even when both groups have some nominal allegiance to a common organizational membership. As much previous research tells us, intergroup cooperation is rarely stable because each group of like-minded employees seeks to dominate, to get the other to do most of the deferring.[1] (Only that way can any group hope to maintain the integrity of its own routines and values.)

Conceptualization of New Business Opportunities at United

United had tried the old sequential method and it had failed: "Under the old model you would just invent something but it would be likely to turn into a business disaster." But management was also sensitive to the need to preserve a substantial voice for the scientific side:

> If you let them, the business people will seek to almost totally define what should be done without much attention to the technical input. That turns out very badly if you are trying to develop a proprietary position that will give you a sustainable technical advantage.

Thus, like many companies with major R&D commitments, United expected the R&D managers to work with their counterpart new-business managers in evaluating and shaping preliminary business objectives and in shaping some kind of early plan and budget. But shared, collaborative, balanced relationships turned out to be more difficult to maintain than was anticipated. The system was designed so that the R&D manager would coordinate with the new-business manager in evaluating preliminary business objectives and plans and resource allocation. In theory this is what was to happen:

> We in R&D do the exploratory work, the "plowing" of the ground, and the "unearthing" of information. We will come across a stone and say "Hey! Does that correspond to a business need?" Theoretically we should then go to the business research people at this point, but that's usually not what happens. They eventually read about our finding in our technical reports, and if they find it interesting will come to us. Then if we and they have the same opinion after having looked at the

"stone," we will try to define it. That is, we will look carefully at this new "stone" from all sides and try to see what it really amounts to.

Blocks to Shared Decision-Making

Surprisingly, in practice there were few inputs from the business people at the critical early, formative stage. The R&D people felt that they could get little guidance from the business people because the latter lacked technical ability:

> The view that they have a broad perspective and can give us guidance isn't true. It's the other way around. When I have gone to them to see whether something we're doing fits into the corporate future, about all they say is "we ought to do more research."

The R&D people end up doing the conceptualization of new business opportunities based on exploratory research pretty much by themselves. In the words of one R&D manager:

> The new-business people can only work with well-worked-through ideas. We take the initiative in making contact but end up being desperate because of lack of guidance. We have to make all the early decisions on direction on our own, including making a lot of assumptions that may be faulty. But at least something gets rolling: you have something.

Differentiated Work Methodologies

R&D people operate in a much more defined work environment than the business research people. Their activities are rooted in the research tradition of the corporation, which has crystalized slowly over a period of many years and has resulted in a stable organizational structure of the department in which the positions of "R&D manager," "group leader," and "bench scientist" are well understood. The structure of the new-business research environment is less well established, the position requirements are much more vague, and there is virtually no research "tradition."

R&D people have an established methodology and procedure well anchored in the scientific method. This determines the way they conceptualize and define problems, as well as their views on how to approach them. Business research people work with largely uncodified methods. This is recognized by the business research people:

> It is difficult work. Nobody really knows how to do it. You need to try experimental approaches and to understand the corporation for which you are doing it. In addition, you must understand exactly the specific situation of each market arena. The rules of the new-business research game are almost completely unwritten.

And in the words of an R&D manager:

> We have a strategy for how to "invent," but we do not have a written philosophy for how to do "innovation." We have no action plans for it. We do have action plans to "invent," and R&D people will continue to invent, because they are basically like a "working machine." The ideal thing, however, would be to have somebody who can say, "This is the business we want to be in, and we need the following leverages, for example, technology, financial, marketing, and so on."

Because of the lack of an established methodology, a way of gathering systematic data, new-business managers cannot easily come up with an analysis to convince the R&D people that they have "discovered" an opportunity. An R&D critic noted:

> Projecting backward from a business need, the business guy ought to be able to say, "This is the window that we need." But our new-business people are not smart enough; they are not trained to do business research. They are completely subjective; they cannot gather systematic data. Business research must be done like any other research project. They satisfy themselves with reading "opinions" in journals, listening to outside people, and so forth. But their level of training is such that they cannot conceptualize; they do not follow a process, a procedure, a methodology.

A new-business research person commented on this difficulty of fully developing new ideas to go beyond "dreaming":

> The real difficult job is to move from the "never-never land," the unbounded optimism of the early phase, as yet imprecisely defined and protected by the corporate muscle, to a phase in which you must narrow down, become tough-minded, become clearly aware of what you need. It is the phase where you have to convince yourself that a concept has validity. Sometimes you have these dreams—for example, you dream up a whole area such as "coastal land management": it is like at a party after a couple of drinks, when you start seeing all these great ideas and every-

thing looks possible. But then the next morning it always seems a little more difficult: What are you going to sell? Who is going to buy it? Why should they buy it from you? That is the tough job, to do that project by project.

But it is not only a question of methodology. The data with which business research people work are less systematic and very often quite subjective.

Industry publications will state, for instance, that users will pay a five-dollar premium per pound of weight saved. But that is entirely deceptive, because these are usually gross averages. The questions are "Who," "What percentage?," "What range?," and so forth. This type of specific information you get only from talking to the customers themselves. You must also make an assessment of the validity of the statements of the customer. For instance, one customer will say that he is wiling to pay five dollars per pound, and you know that is really what he will do. Another guy may say the same thing, but you feel he is actually saying that he thinks there is a 10 percent chance that this is what he would do. So you must try to get more than one reaction to these statements, and try to average them out for each category.

New-business research requires fieldwork. To be sure, there is a type of library research to be done: collecting information on current demand for various products, industry structure, demographic changes, and so forth. However, United was seeking to develop products that would take the place of existing processes and materials used by other companies and consumers, and this meant the firm had to learn the operating details of existing practices and procedures and seek to gain hypothetical information about what it would take to get a user to shift from one material or process to another.

Thus the scientists could enjoy the luxury of a self-contained work environment with most of their pressures coming from their own psyches (curiosity, ambition, achievement norms); their business counterparts felt they were at the mercy of much less controllable external forces. They had to work with potential customers or users who did not really know their future preferences or utilities or how to express them quantitatively. Also, the business people had to respond to an inquiry or request by a customer promptly, dropping everything else to keep the customer involved and interested. A new-business specialist described these differences between the work day of the scientist and himself, jealous of the more shielded world of the scientist:

> The business man operates under different ground rules than the scientist. For the scientist "logic" is the way of life. But business deals with people, and people are not logical. They do lots of things for emotional reasons, and all their decisions are not rational. Scientists are frustrated when they find out that human nature cannot be changed overnight.
>
> Then there is the time dimension. Research reports look pretty much the same from period to period over a number of years. There is just no pressure. In business, the constraints come from the outside; you do not control events.

Therefore the business manager depends upon R&D personnel to help him or her flesh out the potential applications of the new technology. For their part, business specialists seek to find firms and individuals in the marketplace with needs that appear to relate to the new technology and will seek to explore whether and how those needs could be met:

> I have a potential customer who could use such a plastic if it could be used to fabricate x items and cost significantly less than the materials they are now using. Does our new material fit?

At such times new-business research people often initiate to R&D people for help in solving their "urgent" problems. But this is misinterpreted and demeaned by the R&D people, who attribute to business people a "telephone booth mentality"; you just dial R&D for a quick answer:

> Suddenly they will get excited about something and then want immediate answers. They think that if you do some "five-minute" experiments you then know how to make a certain product. They have no understanding of the research process.

How Researchers Want to Interact with New-Business Managers

Researchers recognize that the external system—the world of the user—can have a profound effect on the eventual success of any discovery or laboratory accomplishment. And that system can be quite complex. It may, for example, include very naive users who may not be able to cope with any product or service that doesn't fit their old habits or stereotypes.

> We developed a synthetic material for the home gardener. The product was great, but the marketing people couldn't or didn't find a way to get that user to use just a little; they were always putting in too much.

In this sense, corporate R&D departments are facing the same "system" problems agronomists face in dealing with underdeveloped parts of the world: consumers want to continue their old habits with the new products. New and prolific rice strains are wasted when the degree of moisture in the rice isn't consistent with established tastes for rice. New disease-resistant and prolific hybrid corn gets rejected because farmers want the same kind of corn *stalk* they have always had upon which they have grown beans.

There are also sophisticated users in the marketplace who, given their methods of fabrication and product constraints, have an extensive range of requirements. And the "user" may not be one institution but a whole system of institutions. As Schon pointed out some years ago, an effort to introduce an innovation in fabric cleaning methods would entail dealing with yarn and fabric manufacturers, laundries and cleaners, and equipment and material suppliers to the cleaning industry as well as with the final consumer.[2]

Because of these factors, R&D people are convinced that the management ideal of defining new business opportunities with greater input from the business side cannot really work, because their inputs are useful only if there is a reasonably fixed technological base available.

> For the new model of opportunity definition to be possible, the technology must already exist. Otherwise, the business could not have been conceptualized. Sure, a little piece can be missing, and you look for that. If it works well, then business people become "brokers" between R&D and the market.

Ideally then, the R&D side wants unambiguous, well-supported, quick answers to *their* questions about the market potential of their invention. They would like their business counterparts to say something like this:

> If you could add x feature and subtract y characteristics we have irrefutable data that this new product will sell z millions of dollars worth after w years.

At United the R&D side was critical of the business side for not understanding the market thoroughly enough to provide very specific guidance. In sharp contrast to the stereotype of researchers in industry wanting to be completely unfettered "to do their thing," United's researchers were interested in commercial viability and they wanted more and better inputs than apparently the new business staff could provide. Furthermore, they expected these business specialists to educate future users, where necessary, to gain acceptance for the unique properties of their innovations. And as part of this knowledge of the user, United's R&D people also demanded that they be given realistic information about the limitations of users: "precisely what that group of nontechnically trained consumers can and will do."

Frequently R&D people find that their new-business counterparts don't get back to them with answers to their questions. They feel they get brushed off with comments like, "We'll get back to you on what would be acceptable costs." When no answer is forthcoming, the R&D side develops negative attitudes which may be stated thus:

1. Business types are unreliable; they don't have answers and don't have a methodology for developing them.
2. Make your own assumptions and save yourself the time and aggravation of contacting business development.

When such simplistic assumptions are borne out, R&D personnel become excessively critical and impatient with the value of the business inputs they do receive. They would be eager to have what they consider objective marketing inputs, in contrast to the unsystematic data they claim to receive.

Management Systems

As we noted above, all organizational groups value their autonomy and seek to get "outsiders," typically other departments with which they must work and coordinate, to provide service and support functions and avoid adding constraints. Therefore, it is not surprising that scientists look in vain for service from the management side (i.e., answers to their questions) while simultaneously seeking to fend off demands from business managers.[3]

Business managers typically demand that the research scientists abide by businesslike procedures. However, the researchers are usually vehemently opposed to what they consider the "arbitrary" management systems that the business side seeks to impose on them.

One highly regarded research scientist with a good track record of scientific invention described the effects of the management system this way:

> Written constraints, statements of objectives, milestones, and so on are all dysfunctional. People are optimistic and have a tendency to underestimate the difficulties of getting an array of things done in a given time framework. When the time for evaluation is reached, attention will be paid to what has not been done rather than to what has been accomplished. Management systems are good for controlling things, but they are punitive in essence; they are failure-oriented. The fact is that you cannot predict invention. A prescribed route is always bad for scientists. Invention and scientific work are inherently serendipitous.

Researchers hold to the axiom that the creative process is to a great extent unpredictable; that "invention is serendipitous" and therefore not amenable to administrative routinization and planning. Something can become a failure for the wrong reasons, and something can become a success for the wrong reasons. One scientist provided a striking example of this:

> "Astro-Boy" was a highly successful toy which sold eight million units. Yet it was the outgrowth of a failure in the development of some electronic test equipment.

And then there are those frustrating examples of failures that should have been successes except for extraneous factors.

> We developed a new test for a certain disease. It was a major breakthrough and we thought we had a great new product, and then everything went wrong. One of the basic constituents turned out to be very costly to mass produce. Because the equipment made the germ colonies look very different, there was also resistance from personnel in pathology laboratories.

What Is Being Monitored?

Another point of contention between the two groups in their management systems has to do with their criterion for accomplishment.

While the researchers are not naive about how the corporation measures success in the longer run—it is the profitability of the innovation—in the shorter run they use the criteria of science for measuring a technologist's performance. These are the standards of sound methodology, doing "good" experiments. Scientists investigate questions and problems; once the questions or problems have been defined, the only criteria for judging their work are *methodological* criteria: the professional standards for "good" research. The management system, however, reflects the standards of the business people. They are "result-oriented": the importance of how you got somewhere is relatively irrelevant compared to the importance of whether you got there. As on distinguished scientist-innovator laments:

> Take the high-performance polymer project. One associated research project involved other "preparation" techniques. This work was carried out at the Texas lab before it became my responsibility. It was done successfully three times. Samples were sent out to customers. Everybody was excited about it. Now this program has a major satellite program hung up at the moment, because we have not been able to reproduce the results. We have had people working on it for 3 months, but we haven't been able to figure out a rational reason for the present failure. But that's the nature of research. And that's also why the corporate management system drives people up the wall, because it forces them to write about schedules. Researchers, however, write about things that they have "investigated," rather than about things that they have "done."

Particularly when the laboratory is pushing the state of the art and is exploring poorly understood phenomena, there may not be adequate theoretical understanding, and this problem can be exacerbated by the occurrence of statistically unlikely events. These two factors combined make it very difficult to predict when a discovery will be made or a technical problem solved.

Thus collaboration is impeded by inherent differences in methodology. Science has an explicable, well-regarded set of procedures for validation; in business a less well-honed, difficult to articulate, subjective decision-making process is operative. It is filled with qualifications, such as "If this happens, maybe we can do that" or "We should be able to do that, but not if this occurs."

It is hardly surprising that scientists grow impatient with the pretense that management planning is logical, while business types grow weary with the scientist's drive for perfection and elegance at the expense of stability. Each side thus develops unfair but comforting stereotypes of the other which further impede collaboration.

How Much Fluidity in Product Design?

Scientists fear that the perspectives embedded in the management system encourage marketing people to pressure the researcher to "freeze" further technological development as soon as the new product, process, or system works. However, they are not interested in perfection for perfection's sake:

> Technologists want to focus on the technology; they want to keep changing the product. The marketing guy wants to freeze the product as soon as possible; he does not want to sell one thing this week and next week something quite different.

It is possible that this desire to "freeze" the technology at an early stage grows out of the incentives (or the culture) provided by top management. Obviously in new-venture environments there are great rewards for building your own business. Some more cynical observers believe that this aborts all but perfunctory business research. A top corporate official lamented:

> There is a tendency for the new-business research to stop after about a week. The new-business types want to latch on to a project and develop it quickly into a new business which they can "run."

Instead of an "intelligence" function, business research people have a tendency to perform prematurely a "nucleation" function, focusing their efforts on business development instead of in-depth business research.

Fortunately, experienced, business-oriented new-venture managers have a more sophisticated approach which emphasizes getting something started but maintaining a level of fluidity.

Ironically, the working relationship between scientists and new-business managers is impeded by the same, not contrary, expectations. Nonscientists are critical of the technologists for wanting to elaborate their new product, to "gold plate" it as they say, which means to keep perfecting the innovation. They would like the innovation to be completed and left in a fixed state which would facilitate market explorations and business planning.

60

But research scientists have the same complaint about their business counterparts. They would like clear, unambiguous answers to their questions about the marketplace; precise answers to what new-product characteristics potential customers will demand.

Of course, both sides are being unrealistic in wanting fixed answers too early in the development process. Customers can't give precise answers to hypothetical questions about how much they would prefer more of the x dimension in exchange for less of the y and how that would translate into the price they would be willing to pay. And the target customer group will keep changing as the characteristics of the innovation change or are elaborated in the development process. On the other hand, scientists can sensibly assert that further development *inevitably* changes what is feasible as well as cost-effective. Failure to freeze an innovation at an early stage of development is not primarily a result of the desire to perfect as much as it is the result of new inputs of information. What seems feasible one day will show itself to be unworkable a week later, and some new breakthrough will enable the researchers to add desirable features that seemed impossible before the most recent experiments were completed.

As we noted earlier, this isn't a problem uniquely found in new-business development. All organizational groups seek to gain certainty from outsiders but wish to retain the option of being uncertain themselves—to other outsiders. The reason becomes obvious when one observes intergroup relationships in business organizations. When a given group manifests uncertainty to outsiders, that group's status and power are increased, thus permitting the group to obtain greater resources and greater numbers of perquisites. More important, getting certainty from outsiders is not only a symbol of the outsiders' deference (or respect) for the status of the requesting group, but almost a necessity if the requesting group wishes to maintain its internal routines.

Thus, it is not surprising that scientists want business researchers to give them clear, unambiguous responses when they want them and in the form they need to maintain their schedules and experiments. But the reverse is equally true: business researchers want the scientists to deliver in a timely fashion a clearly defined new product to test in the marketplace.

Both groups' respective need for certainty from the other party and for unchangeable "facts" may be aggravated by the ambiguities of their respective jobs. For the researcher, life is filled with unexpected and insurmountable barriers, where "nature" refuses to release its secrets or perversely contradicts the scientist's most precious hypotheses. Researchers ride a roller coaster consisting of elating highs—technical breakthroughs—and depressing lows—experimental failures.

Meanwhile the business people are also suffering from uncontrollable reality: capricious potential users who either don't know or keep changing their minds and a total market that keeps shifting just as they think they know its dimensions.

Potential Size

Another part of the management system that causes conflict is the emphasis on the potential size of a new market. Business types are indoctrinated with the significance of size: a new business needs to generate sales volume of $50 to $100 million within 5 to 10 years in order to be supported in the context of a large corporation. In contrast, R&D people because of their scientific background come to value the quality or newness of an idea. They also doubt that business managers can identify the truly mammoth potential of an innovation at this early stage in the development cycle. The emphasis on finding only "big winners" discourages the very risk taking that is required for major breakthroughs:

> The difference between marketing and technology people is the difference between "huge" and "new" ideas. There is no encouragement in the system for small exploratory work. Corporate management has all these screens: they want to apply the "rifle" rather than the "shotgun" approach. Great. But it does not encourage efforts oriented toward really new ideas.

Orientation Differences as Between Research and Business

The collaboration and integration of technical and business factors is impeded by the major disparities in orientation that grow out of educational and experiential differences among the participants in this conceptualization process.[4] Another factor that influences the collaboration between R&D people and business people in the conceptualization of new-business opportunities is the quality of the people involved. To begin with, the participants differ in terms of their academic background. Group leaders in corporate R&D typically have a Ph.D. degree in a particular area of science and are very well trained in methodology. They are usually "respected peers" in their field, and are not often caught short of "facts" to support their arguments in person-to-person contact. There probably is some tendency for business and marketing personnel to defer to the R&D professional in face-to-face interactions. Furthermore, R&D people show a slight tendency to patronize their business counterparts.

A senior R&D group leader describes one discouraging confrontation with his business colleagues:

> I feel that my role is to play the devil's advocate. The business types were off and running with the idea that this new compound we were working on would be useful as a catalyst in a certain process. I had to struggle with them to get them to consider the existing scientific evidence that this product would really work that way. In reality the testing had been very poor; what the business people wanted to do was really absurd.
>
> The trouble is that lots of proposals and ideas occur to new-business managers, and they will often be very appealing. But since these people aren't scientists, they can't really evaluate them. It is imperative to check whether they will stand up to a serious technical merit test.

This disdain is not lost on the marketing specialist who views R&D people as "egocentric," "stubborn," and "nonresponsive to the real need of customers." This impedes the collaboration between the two groups. One marketing specialist spoke for many when she said:

> From the perspective of the R&D scientist, the marketing guy is a potential obstruction to his pet ideas. And the R&D type thinks that because he knows the technology he also knows the market better than he really does. As a consequence, the R&D person will tend to fight and dispute the smallest comments made by the marketing type, instead of trying to educate him a little more on the technology. Now, from the perspective of the marketing guy it looks as if the R&D guy is egotistical and has fixed ideas.

Scientists have "probability" answers to problems that occur in development. They often give responses like, "We can say this with 95 percent confidence." Their methodology and training allow them to ask clearer questions that are more relevant to operational procedures and to give more precise answers than their business counterparts. The latter often appear evasive, obscure, or just slovenly in their thinking. They are less likely to be willing to put their opinions in writing, and they have learned to be wary about formally committing themselves. Scientists are used to writing precise reports because their investigative method allows them to say that given the specific context and conditions of an experiment, such-and-such are the results. They can specify which variables were included and which excluded.

It is thus tempting and even easy to criticize the formal business planning and control systems within which scientists are supposed to operate when the basic business data, the premises upon which the plans are based, are all so subjective, anecdotal, and evanescent. In their own sphere scientists are quite formal, for example, in the design of studies, in carrying out procedures, and in writing reports. There is likely to be a more formal hierarchy or rank and status system among technical people among whom there are unambiguous differences in quality of degrees and published research and reputations. All these factors, in contrast to the conventional wisdom, can make scientists both more self-assured and more articulate than their business counterparts.

There seems to be a perception of greater variation in professional competence among people who become business researchers than among R&D people. For example, business research people are often selected on the basis of their availability rather than on the basis of specific unique qualifications for this type of job. "We use 'crutches': we hear about some guy. It is often a word-of-mouth thing."

On the other hand, business research people usually have had substantial, relevant experience before moving to the position they occupy, but these qualifications are often discounted by the R&D people, who see them as "jacks of all trades."

At the same time, R&D people resent the greater credibility that such people seem to have in the eyes of higher management. Thus, giving greater responsibility to business managers for defining new-business opportunities, in contrast to technologists, seems unfair.

> As to the real reasons why they did this, and that is my personal opinion of course, it was because technology people are never given credibility when they come up with a "business" idea. The business people in top management positions prefer the opinion of an incompetent marketing guy to that of a bright scientist.

Inevitably there is competition for the "big chance" between scientific and business people. Each sees the other as less qualified to be the manager of a future new-product endeavor that might follow the initial conceptualization stage. R&D people are very aware of the status of the "big office" attached to becoming the general manager of a new-business organization; they know that corporations reward well those who are "in charge." One scientist who conceptualized a new business opportunity and later became its venture manager described what had driven him:

> It was a significant decision, because I had never operated a business. I had lots of contacts with business people but my career had been in R&D. Nevertheless I decided I would like to have the job of venture manager, and I got it. For me it has been the individual challenge, the seeking of success for success's sake.

Again, the conventional wisdom has scientists in corporate laboratories wanting career lines that stay well within the scientific "community." However, at United, and one would surmise at many other major corporate R&D facilities, an important group of scientists see an upper-management position in their future plans. Riding on the crest of a new business's development is the way to reach such exalted positions. And this brings them into direct competition with the business specialists with whom they are supposed to be collaborating. Obviously this can be a source of tension which injures cooperation.

The differences in perspective, orientation, and background we have been discussing are summarized in Table 4-1.

Improving the Execution of Conceptualization

Fluidity

We have already referred to the distinction between an invention and an innovation. A reproducible laboratory result is a far cry from a viable new product. Understandably there are pressures in a profit-making organization to move forward quickly on promising ideas. But such movement assumes, really presumes, that the critical elements in the total system have been explored. Usually at the conceptualization stage this is not the case, and there are real dangers in freezing the development.

65

Table 4–1
Systematic Differences Between R&D and Business People

Key Dimensions	R&D Personnel	Business Market Research Personnel
Work Environment		
1. Structure	Well defined: • Existence of research tradition • Clearly defined positions	Ill defined: • No real research tradition • Positions less clearly defined
2. Methods	Scientific and codified	Ad hoc and uncodified
3. Data base	Systematic and objective	Unsystematic and largely subjective
4. Work and time pressures	Mostly internal: How long does it take?	Mostly external: How long do we have?
Professional Orientation		
5. Operating assumptions	Serendipity	Planning
6. Goals	"New" ideas: Can it be improved?	"Big" ideas: Does it work?
7. Performance criteria	Quality of investigation	Quantity of results
Quality of Personnel		
8. Educational background	Ph.D.	B.A. or master's degree
9. Experience	Deep and focused	Broad and dispersed
Personal Interests		
10. Career objectives	Become venture manager?	Become venture manager?

The dangers are problems inherent in the system. There is the internal system, elements that are integral to the new product or process and that must be investigated at length. In one of the cases at United we described earlier, a given innovation floundered because one of the major constituents was "too costly" to produce. We are told that invention of an energy-saving motor that presumably sparked the Exxon billion dollar acquisition of Reliance Electric floundered because the innovative motor could not be produced economically—and that was discovered only after a number of years of development.

The external system has the user as its central component. Again, referring to United cases, two proposed innovations floundered because user behavior was more intractable than was presumed. In one case the identification of germ colonies could not be made consistent with laboratory technicians' usual practices and in another consumers could not resist overusing a house plant stimulant.

Yet the most sophisticated and experienced managers, both scientists and new-business specialists, felt that the existence of many unknowns should not deter the establishment of a "test business" when management saw some significant commercial possibilities. Here is a good statement of the rationale:

> As soon as possible we should jump into a test business because that is the method to gather business data. That's how you establish an interface with the outside world. But you must be able to link this test business up with the lab, and use it to test criteria such as "breadth of technology," "number of needs in the market," and so forth, and to formulate objectives and milestones.
>
> The wrong thing is to forget that it is an experimental business: that the results are not dollars but information. Using such an experimental business you open windows. Then you can say to business colleagues, "I don't think that we have the right window," or they can say, "You should reorient your research programs": it becomes an iterative learning process.

Domicile

But where should this embryo business be placed in the corporate structure? There is a strong argument for keeping it within R&D to avoid the imposition of the constraining management perspectives we described above: the conventional planning and control systems, the presumption of stepwise progress and clear sequencing, and the pressures all of these generate to freeze the conceptualization process. The temptation has become strong with the growth of new-venture divisions to swiftly transfer promising new inventions to the jurisdiction of the new-business specialist.

> The test business is not optimized when you establish it as a new business; you need different mechanisms. You need a test business that really belongs to R&D and that is under the jurisdiction of the R&D manager; one that really tests the product. You also need a "nucleation"

function, and here the business must be put in charge of the business development people. But to have the test business is necessary, because business development has no data and cannot develop these data.

Another reason for an R&D domicile is to restrain the natural enthusiasm of the business manager to get the business going. It might be difficult for new-business managers to accept a "test business" as a legitimate experiment. It often is difficult to get business-trained managers to consider good data an end, in contrast to financial results. As we have seen, there may even be a tendency to short-cut an adequate exploration of the demand functions, of what we called the external system, under the pressure to get the new business "rolling." When business managers talk only with themselves, hopes can get exaggerated into firm predictions. Multiple "devil's advocates" are probably a worthwhile antidote to homogeneous groups.

Predicting Future Potentials

We noted that one of the sources of dissent surrounding the contribution of R&D is United's emphasis on major new products, with high sales volume potential. Implicit in this managerial selection process which screens out small innovations is the assumption that one can forecast the future market at this very early stage of the development cycle. That is a highly questionable assumption. Surely no one would have predicted the revolution created by the invention of photocopying. The innovation doesn't simply fit a market; it can create whole new markets.

While very obviously funding can't continue indefinitely, there are some reasons to encourage a longer period of gestation to explore the implications of the innovation for the market. It is highly unlikely that even the most skillful market analyst can estimate the future size of the market for any significant innovation at the early stage of the development cycle. The effort to identify only the most promising innovations too early can have the contrary effect of eliminating all those that are not simply slight modifications of existing materials or products—where the market can be measured quite precisely. The truly innovating product has no market at the outset.

Facilitating Collaboration

It is not surprising or discouraging that the orientation and values of business personnel differ markedly from those of scientists given the vast differences in their background and career experiences. It is only slightly more surprising that each group wants the other to "stand still" (as regards technology, market assessments, and so on) while it retains the option of initiating change and elaboration.

What is crucial is the obvious requirement that professionals from each of the two groups must work more closely than these divergent tendencies would normally encourage. As we have noted, most decisions require simultaneous technical and market inputs, not sequential ones. Each group must be willing to try out or explore modifications that would suit the constraints the other operates under or believes to exist. Such patterns of mutual accommodation and the trust to admit or concede that a favorite parameter might be dropped or may be a variable occur only between employees who share common group membership and common loyalties.

At United simply prescribing that new-business experts and R&D experts would work together at the conceptualization stage could not produce this commonality. In fact, the inherent frustrations of this amorphous period when so much is up for grabs can only encourage each group to scapegoat the other or to insist that the other side must make all the concessions or is "bull-headed." Furthermore, there is competitiveness not only as to who will defer to whom, but as to who will eventually win the real prize: being named as start-up manager of the new-business group.

It may therefore be useful to develop small new-business teams, built around what we have called "test businesses," that precede the formation of a new-business venture group. These teams would have to capture the loyalties of their limited membership by encompassing most of their interactions. It would take a great deal of close, mutually responsive contact to overcome the kinds of differences in orientation we have been describing.

But there is a great deal of experience to suggest that small, somewhat isolated interdisciplinary teams can make enormous contributions and can evoke extraordinary loyalty. If so, special pains would have to be taken to provide physical space and work routines that bring the R&D and marketing specialists closely together as teammates seeking to jointly solve a problem that includes more unknowns than either group can handle alone.

Such close working relations can help to dispel the myths that always abound about the deficiencies of "outsider" groups. As we have seen, contrary to conventional wisdom it is probably more likely that business needs will get short-changed given the greater articulateness of the scientists. Enabling the scientists to see close up the value of business logic and business training in coping with the legitimate systems problems of a new technical idea can help restore the balance between scientists and business personnel.

Summary

Innovation consists of two parts: new technology and a real or potential market. Often the people who know the most about technology are not the most knowledgeable about business opportunities and requirements. The new-venture departments of large corporations seek ways to integrate these two streams of knowledge. In this chapter we have looked at the early conceptualization stage with an emphasis on the sources of problems that can result in faulty initial conceptualization of the product and the market. The precise definition of what innovation the corporation is seeking to develop is by no means easy or obvious. The same technical development can be shaped to go in many directions, and what seems like a simple uniform market is normally a diverse, fragmented set of markets.

On paper it seems easy to plan for the definition of a new product: business-trained managers contribute marketing and production knowledge and science people develop the technology. Rather than doing this sequentially (technology development would be followed by market exploration or vice versa), companies now simply order coordination between simultaneous "technical" and "need" inputs.

In the early stages of the development cycle, when there is an effort to conceptualize a new business there is a need for both a structure and an environment that do not abide by the traditional business logic of milestones, fixed schedules, and budgets. But there is also the need for the close involvement of business-trained and business-oriented specialists who are willing and able to explore market needs and market potential.

A key issue is how to manage these increased inputs by business people during this early conceptualization stage. To be effective, their contributions must *not* diminish the strength of or weight given to the contributions by scientists regarding new-product technology. Otherwise the corporation is unlikely to obtain a technological advantage that can be sustained.

CHAPTER 5

Transforming Projects into Ventures
The Pre-venture Stage

In the conceptualization stage, technical problems were defined and solutions proposed in the light of identified market needs. Forceful and focused development efforts are critical for survival. This requires the formation of an organizational "embryo" for the new business: the development of an administrative structure and the addition of some of the relevant business support functions. Also necessary is the unequivocal demonstration to higher management that a major opportunity exists here both because there is great market potential and the corporation has or can develop the competency to exploit that opportunity.

The Pre-venture Team

Once preliminary business objectives have been defined in the previously discussed conceptualization stage, the corporation usually assigns a project team to undertake market development and further development of the new technology. If these efforts show some success, more concrete business plans will be defined and additional technical and business resources will be added. Engineering and production personnel will be necessary to design a scale-up and to undertake laboratory trials. The administrative structure will become more elaborate.

The Product Champion

The interface between R&D and business people will still be important, but the key activity now is product championing. The product champion is a manager who convinces higher management that the new product or process is feasible and economically attractive and worthy of significant investment.[1]

The early days of a new project are filled with unpredictable barriers and discouragements, and a major requirement for a product champion is the ability to keep improvising solutions with limited resources and continuing doubts that any of this will turn out to be worthwhile. However, even when they are aware of the poor odds the successful champions still remain flexible, adaptive, and optimistic.

> I knew that nobody had been able to pump high-percentage mixtures without risking an explosion. I knew if I could demonstrate that, I could get additional funds for equipment.
>
> There was no way the company was going to fund those expensive processing chambers. I found an engineer who knew all the ins and outs of the company's surplus equipment, and we managed to get a hold of used chambers.
>
> After proving the process was feasible, management thought we should just license the process, but I knew we had recently acquired an operating unit with a product that would benefit substantially from this process.

The product champion must be able to work effectively in a nonprogrammed environment. There is even a sharp contrast to development efforts in the operating divisions which appear much more sequential and systematic. The manager must depend upon dedication, creativity, and even luck and intuition to resolve some of the major uncertainties. One successful manager described his experiences thus:

> The fundamentals of the technology are not clearly established yet. It is

a mixture of empiricism, intuition, and serendipity. It is not like penicillin synthesis, where given my background and in spite of the fact that I have not worked on it for a long time, I still could go to the journals and read about how to do it. But in this area there are so many unexplored parts that it is very different.

I depend upon unpredictable events. In this case, one scientist's knowledge of the "barrier" problem—still a nebulous target—has meshed with the chemical and mechanical knowledge of other scientists in the group. As a result of that interaction, we think that we are able to develop a product that is cheaper than the existing ones.

The product champions have the challenges and the frustrations that are characteristic of any project manager's job. They must deal with a variety of groups over whom they have no control, each of which may be critical to the project's success and each of which has different and often contradictory goals.

A review of one of IBM's early efforts to develop a new small computer [System 3 in 1966–1968] reveals many of these frustrations. The technical product champion immediately had to battle marketing over the type of input the machine would use. Marketing wanted to use what had been a standard type of card input rather than the innovative small card the champion thought was critical to the success of the project. Further the product needed an array of software packages that had to be developed by another unit [industrial marketing] but they were reluctant to commit scarce programming resources to this as-yet-unsuccessful project.

IBM's development process also depends heavily on market forecasts but the group responsible for that activity claimed they couldn't begin their work until that software support was forthcoming and they would know what those costs would be. It was a classic stalemate characteristic of new projects in that the software people wanted some assurances from forecasting that the project had a bright future and the forecasting people needed software costs to make their projections. And then to further confuse things, IBM as a corporation "unbundled" its software from its hardware, rearranging all the constraints and the parameters of the project. Such a milieu demands project managers with enormous endurance and the ability to "massage" a great number of interfaces, repeatedly and perseveringly, to go from one to another seeking to persuade groups to be forthcoming with support or concessions (from rules or standards). As one IBM project manager phrased it, you need one hell of a project to generate the revenues to pay damn good people to fight till they're bloody over a tenth of a percent (difference).[2]

Building the Team and the Project Leader

The conceptualization stage and its linking-up activities are very individualistic. In contrast, technological development work in the pre-venture stage is primarily a collective endeavor. In this respect, the capability of the project leader (usually someone at the "group leader" level in the corporate R&D department) to bring the right people with the right technological imagination and skills on the team is crucial.

Furthermore, as the technology development progresses, additional skills in the engineering and manufacturing areas must be blended with the technological skills of the team. This poses serious management problems for the project leader. When to bring in these functional groups affects the costs of the project. Also, and maybe even more importantly, the logic of the engineering and manufacturing people involves "nitty gritty" details, standard operating procedures, and the like, which are experienced by the technologists as stifling and prematurely dampening to their creative impulses. Yet, if brought in later, the project can run into serious scale-up problems and strategically costly time delays in getting the new product, process, or system to the user. In addition, technology development often turns out to be more complex than anticipated, as new constraints—especially economic ones—are imposed on the project and require trade-offs. In the later stage, when engineering and manufacturing considerations become increasingly important, these trade-offs become all the more complex.

Role of Engineering

One of the most relevant support groups that must be added to the new-venture "embryo" is engineering. Ideally these engineers should be involved from the beginning or at least as soon as market research begins to provide adequate guidance as to market requirements. However, as one project leader pointed out, things are not that simple:

A problem with new-venture management is that you do not do all the engineering thinking in the beginning. It is a time-consuming process, involving a lot of little details. In the beginning you tend to be more concerned with the conceptual aspects; the senior engineer gives guidance concerning what we should not bother with. For instance, we had this problem with the effluence of the gas which made us lose 6 weeks. On the other hand, if we had gone through all the standard procedures it would have been too costly in terms of time too, because you must then commission engineering studies in the corporation, and so on. And that takes a lot of time.

When to involve the engineering people is thus not a straightforward decision. Trade-offs must be made in terms of time and cost. Bringing the engineers in early can be costly in dollars and time. The latter is true, not only because of the time lags involved in asking for and obtaining engineering studies, but also because it may impede the further conceptual development efforts of the technologists, who can get bogged down in small details of little consequence. Beginning serious engineering too soon narrows the range of options the technologists can explore. Some of these small details, of course, turn out to be consequential and may retard the development process in the later stages where scale-up is envisaged. These are part of the costs of bringing in engineering later.

Force Attention to Mundane Problems

While the scientific people will be fascinated with proving the concept, the underlying theory behind the new process or product, they will also be sidestepping a number of what appear to be mundane "nuts and bolts" (or engineering-type) issues that will come back to haunt them. While the latter appear trivial in the light of a new discovery, they can be as difficult and costly to solve as the more basic research. Experienced project leaders learn to factor in engineering inputs with scientific exploration as new market information clarifies the parameters of the would-be new product:

> We finally learned from marketing that we would have to be able to fabricate larger tubes with a 3-centimeter cap, but we could not seem to find any equipment that would keep the cap on. We changed everything, the bottom, top, sides. In fact, it took us a year to work out this "little" element in the technology. It turned out that the cap length is critical, as is a special "crimping" method we developed for which we've submitted a patent application.

76

Preliminary Market Development:
Penetrating the Customer's Organization

Developing new information can be as time-consuming and frustrating on the business side as on the scientific frontier. In contrast to additional market development for existing products, the properties of a truly innovative new product, process, or system are not yet well understood. The market development people are not likely to have a frame of reference that allows them to anticipate the problems that a new user is likely to experience in adopting the innovation. The "need" in the market is often not clearly defined: prospective users themselves do not, and probably can not, clearly specify what their needs are.[3]

If the user is another organization, the market development efforts may require market development people to act as "project managers" for the users, coordinating to some extent the users' R&D and marketing people and putting the users in touch with third parties such as consultants, designers, and vendors. Furthermore, if the user is a complex organization, the new product, process, or system is likely to upset some of its routines and procedures and to create some unanticipated side effects. These unanticipated problems may require a change in the new product, process, or system so as to make it better fit the user organization, or may even lead to a redefinition of the opportunity. Because of the radical impact that the new product, process, or system may have on the prospective client organization, market development efforts may have to take the form of actually devising a custom-tailored strategy for each individual customer, even involving the training of user personnel.

Market development people are often dependent on the customer's interest and willingness to do trials with the new technology. This means that the market developers must be able to penetrate the customer's organization and to make sure that different functional groups in that organization cooperate so as to make trials and experiments (with prototypes of the new product) possible within reasonable time spans. One business manager described some of his experiences with such "beta" (field test) sites:

> You start to look at some of the big companies in the area. Somewhat arbitrarily you start with one of these to build a relationship. You take a big one because you know that larger companies are better for this. But

you need to find a point to contact. Who? One easy way was through one of our operating division salesmen, who made a contact in their purchase department that brought us in contact with the research department. They gave us some components to treat; they would then evaluate our process. But it took them much too long: 3 to 4 months, and then the cycle started all over. It seemed that they were throwing roadblocks in our way. We wanted to get in touch with their marketing people, but we could not get through.

In the meantime, we developed a contact with another corporation. This time I went there myself. We persuaded them to get us in touch with their marketing people. That gave their R&D an incentive and money to do something. Suddenly we found ourselves involved in real market research. They were willing to plan some consumer research while we worked on the design of the component. Meanwhile, and this is important, their R&D did the testing. They were willing to take a risk.

While most technical people underestimate the contribution of marketing, the more successful product champions do not:

You must take the "user needs" into account. That's the gospel. But how do you do it? Those are the real problems. You must know the market; you need very capable market researchers, because otherwise you cannot integrate the right information at the right time. It is very important to sympathize with marketing people. You must see things from their perspective: the problems they will encounter, the forces that impact on the customer. R&D types do not have this exposure; they underestimate these types of problems. It's partly a matter of training; for instance, I am an engineer rather than a scientist. But it's also a question of personality; I like to plan and structure, and to look for the results.

Effective new-product managers recognize the need to develop these unusual skills whereby they pull together resources and groups in the outside organization needed to test out early prototypes of the product or process: the customer's marketing, R&D, manufacturing and quality people—even contractors who do subassembly or fabrication work for the customer.

The market development manager's description of his activities quoted below sounds exactly like what one hears from a product or project manager with minimal authority and lots of responsibility:

This type of work is interesting and frustrating. You want to organize meetings, for instance, but rely on other people to get your stuff together—people from the lab, the customers, and so on. So it is difficult to put together a schedule. How do you do it? You build a plan and consider a number of contingencies. You try to sell the customer and the consultants on the need to perform in time to fulfill your plan. For instance, I will say, "Sure I can give you these containers treated, but if you want them by time x you must give them to me by time y." Also, you offer to help the customer. For instance, the customer may have a design problem. We are the organizing force to bring the designer specialist and the molder together. You need to anticipate problems that the customer encounters, ranging all the way from the esthetics of the design to the molding problems. These things are not our bag, but you must consider them if you want to be effective; you cannot just be "treatment"-oriented.

Gradually it may appear that there are very different market segments, each of which may have special, unique requirements that must be explored individually.

In this one new-product area we discovered that some users might be potential licensees; for others it would make more sense for us to make the product for them; and we also had to approach a third class that would continue to use outside contractors or vendors. Each of these groups of users required a different approach, the development of a special presentation.

If things go well, after years of on-site "testing," relationships will have been established with several customers, a pilot plant will be working, quality control problems will have been handled, and there will be plans for major large-scale market testing. And it is likely that by that time, the real market will look very different from the one originally envisioned in the conceptualization stage.

Interactive Market Assessment

Probably the best type of market development involves an interactive relationship between business and technical people wherein such questions as these are assessed:

1. Is that "need" something that our approach can satisfy?
2. Are we likely to be able to meet that market need with our product or service in a manner that will be profitable to the corporation (potential volume, price)?

The tough part of the process is providing realistic guides for those going out into the marketplace that will help them assess market potential by looking in the right directions:

> Our market development people need more guidance. They come up with uses for this new product that may have a potential of only a half million dollars in sales. In a start-up mode we can't be considering those applications.

Then as technological problems inevitably begin to emerge and designers and technologist seek to evolve prototypes to meet market needs, there are multiple trade-offs:

- Should a different market segment be approached because it looks as though this version of the product is going to be more costly to manufacture than we first thought?
- Or should we look for some design modification that would reduce the fabrication costs?
- Or should we hope for some further technological breakthrough that will lower the manufacturing costs?

Avoiding Too Much Early Success

There is another trade-off at this stage involving upper management. Their attention means that an adequate budget will be available for funding the new project, but when they become too interested, too committed, this can place an uncomfortably bright spotlight on the fledgling project:

> X had to protect his project from too close scrutiny from management. He had to do a lot of tricks to get the time necessary to really develop it. It was a struggle for many years. But he persisted and ended up with one of the best-protected processes in the field.

In another large corporation, innovation has been stifled because top management wants to invest only in what it calls potential "big winners." But when it thinks it has one of these, it scrutinizes the project so much that those involved are inhibited from bringing forth potential difficulties, admitting delays, or making trade-offs. The resulting inflexibility of the project decreases the likelihood that the potential "winnings" will be realized.

Thus top management may want faster results than can be provided or may become disenchanted quickly if something they are watching closely runs into trouble. Technology and business managers prefer less close scrutiny of new projects.

There is always the danger that too much weight will be placed on an early success or breakthrough and that extrapolations will be inaccurate:

> We moved in just a little over a year from the invention of this new technology to a product. We got it installed in a major user's facility. What we didn't realize was how unusual this installation was. Just by chance we had encountered a bottleneck operation and our process increased output in this operation's sector by 6 percent and also controlled pollution. It turned out that this product didn't work that well at all in plants of a different scale. We had started with four aces in our hand and we expected at least three next time. Instead there were none; we should have taken more seriously some of the problems we had seen in our earlier studies. What we finally learned was that our first experience of success had been the anomaly.

Thus premature commercialization can lead to false starts. Unique problems, creative trial and error, and happy accidents—the catalytic effect of unanticipated phenomena that scientists often call "serendipity"—are all important components of the technology development for all really new products. Sheer "good luck"—the occurrence of an improbably positive result in the early stages of technology development—turns out to be quite important, because it allows a project to "show something" and thereby to generate further support from management as well as the motivational energy to "find out why it worked." Yet "good luck" can also be deceptive and may delay the awareness of real flaws in the new product, process, or system.

Product Announcements

Product champions face another dilemma. There are some obvious advantages to issuing a "semiofficial" announcement concerning the characteristics of the new product. At times this can have a preemptive effect in the market, discouraging potential competitors who are somewhat further behind in their development efforts or who are considering initiating a development effort. The willingness to make a public commitment also demonstrates to top management that the development team is enthusiastic, united, and self-assured about their ability to meet their projected schedule.

The negative side of all of this is that the announcement is a commitment of sorts and it can cause the project people to diminish their efforts in both market research and technological development. Further trade-offs and project modifications may be prematurely discouraged. There may be too heavy an emphasis on selling and entering a new market before the product is really ready.

Support for "Need Pull" Versus "Technology Push" Projects

"Need pull" cases, especially, face the hazard of too much higher management scrutiny too soon, because such projects tend to take off relatively quickly. Because of management's greater awareness of what goes on in such projects, higher-level support is usually more readily available. However, higher management's patience tends to be limited and its interests change fairly quickly, giving the pre-venture team relatively little time to produce some quick success demonstration project to enhance its credibility. "Hiding" thus has survival value in the pre-venture stage, because technology development invariably takes longer than expected.

"Technology push" projects don't have it that easy. In fact it is also very difficult to get top management to commit resources to these projects. Almost by definition such projects are seeking to accomplish an objective that has been defined as extremely difficult. In fact, to date it has probably been impossible.

> We think we discovered a method of controlling a very unstable chemical process. But to demonstrate feasibility we will need to acquire pumps worth $50,000, and they probably can't be used for anything else if this particular method doesn't work. Management is reluctant to put up that much funding for a long shot, but if we don't get it there will be no way of proving that we're onto something.

Thus this can become a vicious circle: money is hard to get until it's possible to show feasibility, but the project needs the money for that purpose. Hence, a major role of project champions, as we noted before, is to find existing resources that can be converted after being begged, borrowed, or stolen.

The Interaction of Technology and Market Development

In the R&D department at this point in time, there are usually two major groups. One is exploring and pushing current applications of the product or service that has been identified as the vehicle for growth by the product champion. There is also a more technically oriented group that is continuing to explore the underlying technology.

In Chapter 3, we observed that technology push projects experience different problems in conceptualization than do need pull projects. These problems must be dealt with in the pre-venture stage as the market and technology development processes begin to have an impact on one another. Technology push projects start naturally with a focus on the technology development. As information is produced by market development, these projects must reconsider their technology development efforts. Often, in fact, the result of a clarification of the market needs is a redirection of the technological efforts toward applications that are more difficult than the one with which the project started out, and/or to entirely new applications that suit the average customer rather than the atypical customer. Sometimes a complete redefinition of the opportunity (e.g., to a service rather than a product business) may be in order. Figure 5–1 illustrates the redirection of the technology development process.

Figure 5–1
Market Development Redirects Technology Development

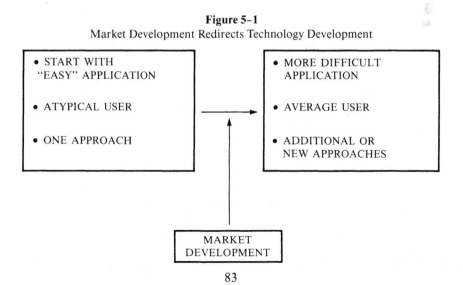

The market development efforts thus lead to a sharper focus and result in pressures from the business side on the R&D side to be responsive to customer problems and demands.

Once the product, process, or system that is required in the light of market development efforts is more clearly identified, the business side typically wants to freeze it. At the same time, however, pressures are exerted from the R&D side, especially from the people already working on second-generation technology and applications, to get further market guidance for their work. The business side is reluctant to provide this because of its desire to now focus on the established product/need combination. This conflict in expectation (freezing versus continued technical development), already discussed in Chapter 4, continues to create tensions between R&D and business people in the pre-venture stage.

Need pull projects, on the other hand, start naturally with a focus on the market development aspect. However, as the technology development efforts begin to take shape, the initially vaguely identified "need" often must be redefined as a result of clearer insight into technological limitations (in terms of providing a "sustainable advantage") and/or realization of limited commercial potential.

Increased insight into the technical and economic constraints attendant upon the development of a new product leads to a clearer definition of the inherent opportunity connected with it, which provides the market development people with better search guidelines and exerts pressure on them to define this opportunity in more concrete terms. However, there may be difficulties in developing adequate momentum to follow through on the painstaking technological side of the development effort. These need pull projects will often lack an obvious product champion since they have not begun with a technology breakthrough. Thus at this point the organization can flounder without a strong directing hand, and there will usually be a search for someone who will act as a "champion." Figure 5–2 illustrates the redirection of the market development process.

As technology development becomes more important in these need pull projects, the R&D people feel they can make demands on the business group to be more concrete in defining the market opportunity in regard to which they are seeking to invent-to-order an appropriate technological breakthrough. The response of the business side is often to counter with pressure for faster technological development, even when their own definitions of the market are still in

Figure 5-2
Technology Development Redirects Market Development

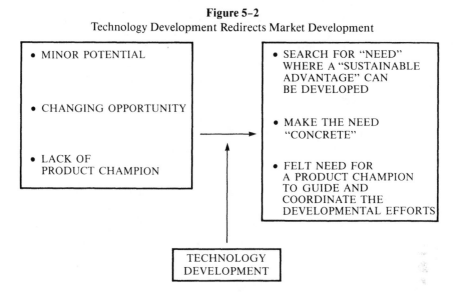

flux. Needless to say, these pressures and counterpressures add to the tension inherent in these interdisciplinary relationships.

Managing the Interface Between R&D and Business Research People in the Pre-venture State

At United pre-venture teams traditionally had stayed under R&D jurisdiction by simply transferring the project from the research laboratory to a scale-up site and adding marketing people, engineers, and consultants. Increasingly, however, pre-venture teams were set up in matrix-type fashion, with business research and R&D people reporting administratively within their own department, but with the R&D group leader also simultaneously reporting to a business manager heading up the pre-venture team. Figure 5-3 illustrates such matrix structures.

Functioning of the Pre-venture Team

Typically, in the new matrix set-up, the business manager is the team leader whose responsibility is to ask the technical staff, "Can the new product be improved technically?" and query the business peo-

Figure 5-3
The Structure of a Pre-venture Team

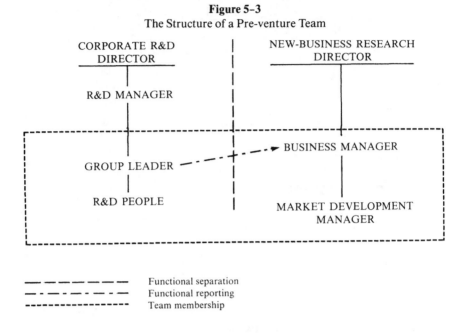

——— ——— ———   Functional separation
— · — · — · — · —   Functional reporting
----------------   Team membership

ple, "Is it acceptable to potential customers?" The market development manager scans possible new-product applications, seeking to discard applications that represent markets that are too small to pursue. The technology development people are working simultaneously on adapting the new-product technology to marketplace requirements and also on more basic research that is less applications-oriented.

In describing the cooperation between the business and technical components of the team, one enthusiastic technical manager noted:

> We really are the trouble shooters for the marketing people. When a customer gets into some unanticipated trouble using experimental material from our group, we drop our more long-range development work and jump in to get an answer back. While the bench scientist often sees this as wasted effort, we have to do this sort of thing. After all, our project needs commercial results in terms of dollars of sales. That's your credibility and is the way to convince management.

In fact, in a well-run project there will be a high frequency of such initiations from business people to technical specialists as the customers' needs begin to be clarified. There will be lots of special tests to run and estimates of production costs under varying conditions to calculate.

A market development manager indicate how she tries to get the R&D people to focus their efforts on helping the emerging business:

A crucial thing is to define the needs of the users; for example, the level of moisture in the atmosphere, whether operators will beat the thing with a hammer, the stress requirements, and so forth. I tell the researchers that we want to sell 600,000 units of a particular part. Then I ask them how they think it should be made, rather than try to tell how it should be made. If they answer that question, then you create a vested interest on their part, a commitment to "their" contribution.

This same manager emphasized the importance of creating a direct communication link between potential customers and the R&D people to increase the latter's understanding and commitment:

We always hope to get good communication between our organization and the customer, because otherwise we run the risk of spinning our wheels, of making things that are not designed in the right way.

That's why I try to make sure that there are direct visitations and interactions between the technology people and the customers. The technologists need to taste the flavor of the customers' needs themselves. Also, that leads to a better assessment of the customers' needs because different people have now interpreted them and discussed them. It avoids your becoming trapped in an optimistic or pessimistic mood when you make the assessment.

Unfortunately, in some organizations that consider themselves innovation oriented, contact with customers is discouraged for technologists. The business specialists are reluctant to share this source of status and ideas with their counterparts.

One business manager emphasized the importance of "proximity" of the team, because there are virtually no set procedures: everything changes all the time:

You need the proximity. Otherwise you are handicapped. There are always a large number of reasons that you can think of, it seems, for not going to the other person. And that's even easier when you are physically separated.

You are always working on something new. It takes a while before everybody can understand, and by that time the situation changes again.

For this reason, the business manager, the technology manager

(R&D manager level), and the market development manager were given offices next to each other in the same building. On the other hand, the technical development manager (group leader level) and the R&D people at the operational level were situated in the scale-up site 45 miles away, and that created problems.[4] Not only did it create problems between the business side and the R&D side, it also created potential difficulties among the R&D people at different levels:

> The communication between here and the lab is not so great because of the geographical distance. That's somewhat of a problem, because you need to kick around ideas. It is fortunate that the group leader and I had the opportunity to work together before, so the necessary rapport had been established.

The technical managers are also sensitive to their need for business guidance, as seen in one technical development manager's description:

> We need marketing input on an ongoing basis—liaison. Unfortunately, we are often left working in the dark. Also, the targets keep moving. Marketing people do not put the targets down in writing; they do not commit themselves. It's not enough to talk about cost competitiveness; they must specify what cost competitiveness means precisely in dollars and cents terms. For example, we are working on a particular component that weighs 100 grams; we know that it needs to be lighter; we need to know how much it can cost. Now marketing people are used to doing the cost studies. For 6 months we have asked them for some input on cost. We would ask them, "Is 70 grams light enough?" and they would answer, "Maybe." So we did not know what the target is. And that is important. Because if the marketing people say that a project is not good, then it is hard for upper technical management to convince corporate management that it is good. Just a few weeks ago did we start to get some of the information we needed.

Interestingly enough, some problems arise because the R&D people get ahead of the business people. Business managers, once they have discovered a reasonably good opportunity, focus nearly all their efforts on exploiting it so as to develop a sufficient growth rate to keep higher management interested. Emphasis on the present or most obvious opportunity, if not tempered, could foreclose the exploration of what might be more fruitful future technological opportunities in a given new venture.

From Pre-venture to Venture: The Major Transition

Successful technical and market development during the preventure stage brings a project to the point where higher corporate management will consider its graduation to full venture status. Such a transfer provides a major impetus for a project because it now becomes an embryonic business organization with its own venture manager, budget, and profit and loss (P&L) statement. Higher management has now signaled its intention of letting the project grow into a complete new business that will later be fitted into the corporate operating system. At the same time, the project leaves the protective environment of the corporate R&D department and the commercial potential of the new product, process, or system must now be demonstrated.

Because of the ambivalent corporate attitude toward radical innovations it is often difficult to develop clear policies and procedures to guide the new project's "graduation." Each case is perceived to be different, and not surprisingly uneasiness and uncertainty are found on the part of higher management regarding how to approach the transition of a project from pre-venture to venture status:

> There are no hard and fast rules for this. When do you do it? The textbook answer is when the new product, process, or system starts meeting its sales forecast for a year and when it has a realistic 5-year plan that it can realize. But there are too many unknowns for the textbook answers to hold. It's different for each venture; it depends on how we are going to do it, on what the business strategy is going to be.

Given the degree of uncertainty and lack of uniformity, the importance of "championing," meaning managerial activities that create the conditions under which continued corporate support for a project is likely to be forthcoming, is not surprising.

It is also not surprising therefore that subjective factors play a significant role at this stage. Top management's decision will be influenced by articulate, persuasive sponsors who can make the case for adding this innovation to the company's product/service portfolio.

Organizational Championing

We have termed these the organizational championing activities. It is the complement to the product championing activities we described

89

earlier in this chapter. The product champion conceptualizes a technical vehicle by means of which he or she asserts that the corporation can develop a viable new product or service. The product champion sees the relationship between scientific developments and market needs and can conceptualize the chain of events that lead to the development of a new product, process, or system with significant commercial potential.

In contrast, the organizational champion understands the purview—that is, the fields of interest and strategies of the corporation at this particular point in time. The organizational champion is able to relate the parameters and potential of this new venture persuasively to the ultimate goals of the corporation. Insofar as the new venture doesn't fit snugly into current definitions of the corporate portfolio and domain of strategic activity, the champion/sponsor must be able to justify an extension of the accepted fields of interest that will legitimate this new venture. He or she is the one who establishes the link between the new venture and what we have called in Chapter 3 the "fabric" of the corporation.

Organizational championing is often performed by the head of new-business development for the corporation, but it could also involve some other upper-level manager who is willing to risk his or her reputation on the highly visible sponsorship of the relatively untried and radical new innovation.[5] Obviously, such an organizational champion will be an executive in a position to observe a number of new ventures and who can judge their relative potentials for maturing into vigorous, viable new businesses. Beyond that, the organizational champion must be able to articulate a coherent strategy for the nascent new business which will appear both credible and appealing to top management.

These cognitive and behavioral skills go well beyond the technical insights, energies, and enthusiasms of the product champion. Most important of all is the ability to make a convincing case when selling the venture to top management. The successful organizational champions explain the technical perspective and conceptions of the product champion to senior executives and go from that to the strategic implication of the new, emerging business and its potential to become a multiline business. Less successful organizational champions don't see or can't communicate this broader gestalt of the new venture nor can they conceptualize the related products that will strengthen the chances of the new venture's achieving a "critical mass."

Timing

Timing can be critical. There are temptations and inducements that encourage sponsors to push for full venture status too early:

> If it "graduates" too soon, the new venture will probably be of marginal size—in terms of sales volume—and will attract a lot of scrutiny in terms of financial performance by the "management committee." That close a scrutiny may not be good for its further development.
>
> On the other hand, there will be strong pressure to get that venture status because the manager involved with the innovation can then get the perquisites associated with an autonomous project: being recognized as having the status of a general manager, getting a big office, and the like.

There are dangers in restraining the push for new-venture status too long as well. To do this impedes provision for adequate financial support and for obtaining the kind of track record that will lead to the product obtaining free-standing status. Such delayed projects, in the words of participants, get "screened to death."

Conclusion

Innovations in large corporations go through a period of adolescence prior to the time they are accepted as "young adults" with some organizational autonomy. During this pre-venture try-out period a business team seeks to run the new product or service as though it were a new business coping with marketplace problems, while continuing to work on product development. The problem at this stage of the development cycle is to balance the requirement that a good test of the new product's potential marketplace success be done (by actually selling the product) with the need to have some flexibility in the parameters of the new product and to make any necessary changes. Achieving compatibility between what appear to be incompatible activities and requirements is the key challenge for managing a venture's development in this stage.

CHAPTER 6

Establishing a One-Product Business
The Entrepreneurial Stage

The senior managers of the newly minted venture must make several types of strategic decisions that will have a profound effect on its early history. Their location in a larger corporation and their dependence on top management for nurturance as well as the inherent uncertainties of the early life of a new business influence these strategic choices. The most important decisions appear to involve the new venture's rate of growth, its internal functional development, and the addition of complementary products and services. In turn these relate to some difficult issues involving planning the careers of those involved with the new venture.

Rate of Growth

There are obvious pressures that motivate venture managers to seek a fast takeoff. From the point of view of the corporation, the opportunity costs associated with investments in a new venture will often seem high because, by definition, there is little experience by which to judge the market or the rate of progress. Most new ventures do not have an indefinite period to prove themselves, even though established products are allowed many "down" periods. (Only in periods of severe capital stringency will some well-established but consistently poorly performing business be sold.)

We observed a great deal of what could be called "strategic forcing" designed to help the new venture to secure an impressive toehold in the market.[1] The presumption is that by setting and then achieving difficult growth goals, the new-venture manager's internal staff will be pressured to work with extraordinary determination and top management will be reassured about the future of the new venture.

If successful this can lead to an upward spiral consisting of more top management support and thus greater corporate investment in the venture, which in turn should allow for still better growth. This will help establish the new venture's "track record" and justify continuing generous support.

The specific method of doing this was stated boldly by one new-venture participant:

> Our way of dealing with top management is to double our size each year. We also seek to acquire assets that can't be easily disposed of. This discourages top management from getting rid of us, and we might even be able to relax if we have one bad year.

Of course, if the forcing doesn't work, a downwardly sloping spiral can emerge in which failure breeds failure. When projected sales levels aren't reached, R&D budgets get slashed. An unanticipated technical problem can't be fixed because there aren't adequate funds to hire the people to work on that problem. In one case we observed that a new venture that had lost some of the confidence of top management received additional burdens:

> We had a highly technical and unusual product that required a sales staff that could build confidence with the customer. When we ran into these problems, top management no longer allowed us to hire our own sales staff. We were assigned some from one of the operating divisions. They were used to working "on the golf course" and through socializing and were incapable of dealing with a product that still had growing pains.

Forcing has another potentially negative aspect. It leads the venture to try to sell products or services before it may be able to produce them well. At times the new product or service may be at a stage in which each installation ought to be monitored closely to learn both

93

customer experiences and product idiosyncrasies. Rather than seeing these early sales as controlled experiments, they are made as though both the market and the technology had been fully explored. The result is often that the back-up R&D staff is in the position of falling behind and trying to catch up—seeking to remedy flaws in the systems that have been or are about to be sold. And these defects in the new products will have repercussions in production that will require still more scarce technical inputs. Unfortunately many of the quick "fixes" will be less optimal than solutions to design and manufacturing problems made under less duress.

Selecting the Venture Manager

Given the rate of growth anticipated and required by the corporation, it becomes highly likely that a technical manager who has worked closely with the new product during its inception will be chosen as venture manager. Often this will be the "product champion" described earlier, who has become the product's most visible proponent and can thus provide the fastest takeoff. Also, because these are radical innovations for the organization and there is little past experience to guide decision-making or by which top management can evaluate what is occurring, it seems quite natural to allow the expert who has been absorbing most of the uncertainty in the project's development to continue.

Such a choice is also consistent with the reward system implicit in the career paths the corporation establishes. Upwardly mobile managers in corporate R&D look enviously at the direct rewards, "perks," and status associated with general management. They want to move over from the professional to the managerial side and they see a promising new product as the vehicle for their growth as well as for a new business's growth. But, of course, just as the best worker or craftsperson doesn't make the best first-line supervisor, the best technical person, even when highly motivated, may not have the people skills and managerial discipline to run a new business.

Organization and Administration

In the rush and push to gain that critical sales volume threshold, it is tempting to neglect organization building. Not only are dollars and time required to build an administrative system that will operate reliably to support the new business, but entrepreneurs are tempted to coordinate everything themselves.

For most entrepreneurial new-venture managers, this is a self-conscious "strategic neglect"[2] of organization building in favor of single-minded pressure for sales growth (and quick technological "fixes"). This is accomplished by the close supervision and continuous involvement of the entrepreneur/venture head. Such individuals may justify their concern with every detail and a reluctance to delegate responsibility thus:

> I have to show I can make a profit. I must monitor all the variables because a profit is made by a small gain here and one percent there. The larger the business the more important this becomes because there are then hundreds of variables.

The Management Team

At this early stage in the life of the new business it is presumed that there is no need for costly specialists for manufacturing, purchasing, or engineering. There is also a tendency to use cast-offs from the operating divisions. These may well be highly ambitious, more entrepreneurially oriented managers who didn't fit the mold of more routine operations. They become jacks-of-all-trades who know a little bit about a number of specialties and can be assigned work that crosses or falls between more traditional job boundaries.

While this flexibility can be very useful in this early, turbulent period, it can also be a handicap. Lacking either professional qualifications or identifications, these managers are unlikely to push for the development of administrative routines. While expediency is fine in the earliest days of the venture, continued reliance on ad hoc solutions and the absence of set procedures can be a major handicap in the development of an efficient business. Furthermore, the absence of some inherent system of managerial specialization only encourages continued close supervision and intervention by the head of the venture. Since there are no predictable, routinized decision channels, there are inevitably more apparently "big" decisions to tempt the entrepreneur to try to have a say in everything. He or she ends up running faster and faster in a futile effort to control all the activities of the various functional support areas.

95

New-Product Development

The price paid for this truncated development of the business is often most forcefully shown in the neglect of new-product development. Strategic forcing inevitably focuses management's attention on *the* most promising vehicle for rapid growth. While the existing technological innovation is the obvious candidate, it is ironic that a business based on innovation may begin to ignore the importance of continuous innovation for continued, healthy growth.[3]

> An innovative new medical product, spawned within the research labs of GE but sold off to the developers to run as a private business, was nearly aborted when a competitor developed a much lighter piece of equipment. The viability of the new venture was only assured after a major product change introduced a great deal of miniaturization that enabled the product to compete effectively with the newly introduced other machine.[4]

There will be many such threatening developments in the marketplace, and there should be many additional opportunities generated by the corporation's scientists and technical staff. In the organization we studied, once the venture achieved independent status there was a new division of labor in R&D. Developing and perfecting the product or service that generated the venture became the responsibility of an R&D division that was under the control of the general manager of the venture. Corporate R&D was supposed to contribute technological development in *related* fields and back-up support where needed.

Here is how one new-venture scientist sought to describe the respective jurisdictions of the two technical groups:

> Corporate R&D should help the business only in fundamental areas, like physical chemistry, where there is a chance that basic patents can be obtained. Corporate R&D should not be addressing a marketplace problem unless the new-venture management has specified the criteria for success. Venture R&D should have the responsibility for developing new things. Of course it can buy some of corporate R&D's time.

Realistically, it is not going to be easy to find that balance between "fundamental areas" possibly leading to basic patents, in which corporate R&D provides support to venture R&D, and areas that are solely the province of the new venture's R&D group.

Of course, these aren't watertight categories and each will influence the other. New work in related fields may hold the solution for an unanticipated glitch in the current technology, and the work of the new-venture R&D group could stimulate the centralized corporate group to try some new directions.

Regrettably, a formidable barrier soon emerges to separate the two groups; this is quite understandable. The venture R&D people feel the need to develop their own identity in the face of the established prestige and size of their mother department. But these adolescent strivings for independence can be carried too far:

> They don't even talk with us. It's ironic, they fund our work for them in the corporate labs but the technology we developed wasn't acceptable.
>
> We often have the sense [in the corporate lab] of having to do work for them in spite of their lack of interest. We even have to seek to anticipate what their problems and needs are going to be in order to be ready to respond and act when it becomes necessary.

The corporate lab professionals can make the situation worse by their feelings of superiority. They are quick to point out that high-quality personnel may be in short supply in the venture. In the words of one corporate scientist:

> You find two extreme types of people in new-venture groups. There are some who are aggressive and intelligent, who are turned on by the challenge of getting something to work. And you also have the ones who were out of a job and easy to pick up for the new business. Most corporate R&D people would not want to work in that venture environment.

Some of these comments are too critical. In better-managed new ventures there is real concern for quality research. In the words of one group leader:

> Both John and I—if I may say so—have been able to excite people. They know that we want to establish identity for the R&D groups here. We want to publish papers, develop patents, have meetings and conferences here, and so on. So we have been able to bring some good people with us.

But as it tries to reach the objective of establishing identity, the venture R&D function runs into some problems. First, there is poor operations support because of the lack of administrative development.

> It's somewhat frustrating for me to deal with business people; it's a little aggravating. I ask myself why the purchasing and accounting department cannot be set up correctly. Why don't they take the existing corpo-

rate systems and adopt them here? The corporate R&D was just a much more supportive environment; you were sheltered there and got serviced properly.

Second, the other functions, especially the emerging operations and manufacturing functions, still interfere a lot with the research work of the new R&D function.

> It is rough going to keep my people happy. They get tired of "fire fighting" in production; it's frustrating. So my biggest problem at the moment is to balance the emotional states of my people. They have high demands; it's very difficult.

Thus it is not surprising that this uncomfortable and somewhat vague distinction between the jurisdictions of the two R&D groups impedes an adequate response to the "aging" of the venture's premier new product. The very innovation that would not have occurred without major inputs of technical talent may now be starved for additional inputs of comparable talent.

The Limits of Strategic Forcing

Strategic forcing requires a conscious strategy of neglect of some things to capitalize most quickly on the growth possibilities of one new product. By most corporate standards, this amounts to an almost reckless neglect of the time-consuming but necessary activities associated with building and living within the constraints of an administrative structure.

For a while, if the product has reasonable potential strategic forcing works, but it has sown the seeds of its own destruction by its excessive short-run view. Particularly by failing to address the continued flow of new models and new products, strategic forcing threatens the viability of the new enterprise. But even where the venture continues to grow, corporate management comes to recognize the structural incapacities of the venture and places the blame appropriately on the venture manager.

It can be both ironic and sad to observe that such managers, who have been motivated by "the system" to grow rapidly at the expense of good organization and longer-run concerns, are then lost to the system when these shortcomings become apparent. Their demise may even occur at the very time that the venture achieves self-sustaining growth.

Top management is likely to say that they needed a technically trained and oriented manager to get the venture going but then a "real" manager should take over who can build structure and systems. There is no necessary conflict between technical expertise and general management ability. However, it is likely that the technical manager who built the venture came straight from a purely technical management assignment. This individual was promoted because of his or her knowledge of the technology and accepted because he or she sought a vehicle to rise to a general management position.

In allowing this selection criterion and these inducements to operate, management is also bound to provide compensating support and training to encourage the development of these broader managerial skills. Regrettably, the opposite often occurs. Wanting quick results to allay the anxieties associated with an investment decision that was probably filled with uncertainty, top management continues to tolerate what is probably self-destructive behavior from the venture manager. This leads to high personnel costs, both personal and organizational.

Strategic Building

For the venture to sustain growth there must be a master strategy for operating within the broader new-business field in which the new venture will eventually be only one element. Evolving and implementing such a strategy usually requires the agglomeration of other new products and services "around" the original innovation. These may come from new technologies being developed outside the corporation, in its corporate laboratories, or they may already be in existence in the operating divisions. The needed strategic skill here is the ability to conceive of a larger business thrust into which a number of initiatives can fit and reinforce each other.

Strategic building typically takes place at the level of the new-business-development (NBD) manager (the venture manager's manager). Managers at this level evaluate, judge, and select projects and encourage entrepreneurial managers of the selected new ventures in their strategic forcing efforts. Strategic building implies seeing the

99

wider implications of the project's success, understanding what the key to that success is, and being able to use that understanding to widen the scope of the venture activity. Here is how this happened in one of the ventures we studied:

> In 1974–1975, Dr. K. came up with the idea of a "systems approach," and expressed the need to move things toward consolidation. At the same time, the burgeoning medical equipment venture was developing a capability to do that, so the corporation wanted to coalesce all its medical activities using the venture as an umbrella.

The venture became the administrative umbrella under which otherwise unrelated medical projects (like a "blood-banking" business) could be agglomerated, thus capitalizing on development activity in other parts of the corporation and thereby creating further impetus for the health field in the corporate context. Said one of the participants:

> You must realize that, in fact, the diagnostics markets and the blood business are quite distinct and different. However, it was the genius of Dr. K. to attempt to get a better focus by bringing all the capabilities relevant to the medical field existing in the corporation under one management. That is to say, the refrigeration know-how of the Cryogenics division, the plastics know-how of Packaging Products, and the electronics know-how of Medical Equipment.

While this conception is more likely to be the product of a higher-level executive in the new-business arm of the corporation, it is dependent upon the existence of a solid base of success in the initial venture. It is this base that produces the credibility and track record that will encourage corporate management to provide continuing and generous support. But even more important, the initial venture provides the basic learning from which a strategy can be constructed. Since these are radical innovations, by definition the corporation does not have a reservoir of knowledge about the market or the technology. Only after that learning has been acquired can a sensible, realistic strategy be enunciated.

Managerially, then, the tough problem is—as is the case with many managerial challenges—that you can't do B until you've learned to do A. However, it is very easy to get caught up in doing A and then become reluctant to shift attention from A to B—after so much emphasis has been placed on A (forcing) to devote major attention to B (building).

100

The existence of this master strategy or design pays a number of dividends to its author, who, as we have said, is frequently a senior manager in the new-business development group of the corporation. The strategy serves as a guide to the subordinate venture manager and his or her key managers. Like any policy, rule, or standard, when it is well conceived the articulated strategy takes the place of continuous involvement of senior management in decision-making. This frees up time that can better be devoted to working "up the line" with top corporate management.

The plan also serves a crucial function in those relations. Its very existence—when accepted—mobilizes support with corporate management. The relationship of the new venture to the larger corporate strategy can now be enunciated. Having a well-conceived strategy also allows the new-business sponsors to "stay ahead of the game." They are now able to anticipate the questions a sophisticated corporate management will ask. In addition, they can make demands on corporate management that will look reasonable and gain justification by their contributions to fulfilling the previously accepted and therefore now-legitimated strategy. In the words of one astute middle-level manager:

> New businesses have growth problems that the corporation does not easily understand. So, if you don't have a clear strategy you only ask them what you know they will be able to understand. But then you are always behind, and that will destroy your credibility.

When problems arise in connection with the new venture, they can be tackled in the context of this recognized new field to which corporate management has become seriously committed. Such a base or presumption provides a much more supportive environment than a series of ad hoc reappraisals.

An articulate introspective manager with substantial experience in this role defined his task this way:

> First, I look for demonstrated performance on an arbitrary tactic—sometimes this is not even the right one. For instance, perfecting this one application of our new technology may not be the right move, but it can be done and one can gain credibility by doing it. So what I am really looking for is the ability to predict and plan adequately. I want to verify my manager's claims to predict and plan. So you need a "demonstration project" even if it is only an experiment.
>
> The second thing that I look for is the strategy of the business. That is the most important milestone. The strategy should be attractive and

workable. It should answer the question of where you want to be in the future and how you are going to get there. It is important for two reasons. First, once you have a strategy (and you can answer those questions and you can verify a piece of it through a demonstration project) you can give strategic guidelines; you can let people make more independent decisions. That builds momentum, and you don't have to go to top management every day; so it's also very important from an operation viewpoint. Also, it allows you to plan. And that in turn allows you to go to the corporation and stick your neck out.

Entrepreneurial Versus Business Values: Career Problems

We have already seen that the corporation engaged in radical innovation may be seeking contradictory things. It wants the super-fast growth and bold, personal commitment associated with the entrepreneurial spirit. At the same time—or shortly thereafter—it wants solid business development including a structure with responsible functional specialists and a carefully conceived business plan. At times, excessively enthusiastic entrepreneurial efforts will embarrass corporate management or even impinge on the more carefully regulated operating divisions. The usual result is an effort to "harness" the entrepreneur. But these efforts usually fail because in terms of both selection criterion and the earlier reward system, the venture manager was trained to go all out. Harnessed entrepreneurs become like the proverbial "wild ducks willing to fly in formation": a contradiction in terms.

One careful observer of a number of new ventures described the problem well:

> In our company, the technical entrepreneur is the first in line to become the general manager of a venture because he is considered the "expert." I feel that this comes from the fact that we haven't been able to separate the phases in the development process clearly. We need to define much more clearly what is involved in the transition from an individual effort to a management effort. We need to define these phases better. Other corporations have the same problem: when to move the "entrepreneur" out and bring the "manager" in.

And, as a colleague of the first observer noted:

> We are not psychologically structured to give the entrepreneur a free hand. The whole administrative and productive machinery is set up for

large activities. Lots of reports are needed; everybody wants to know what the entrepreneur is doing, not just that he is "doing well."

A major managerial dilemma then is how to use the internal entrepreneur. One solution would be to stop using "product champions" in the role of venture manager. We have noted already, however, that efforts to get more business-oriented people to take on the venture manager role conflicted with the "radical" character of these innovations. They require the intense commitment of someone who knows that he or she is going to be able to follow through on the new product's development. In addition, whatever their background the venture managers in the embryonic business stage must perform the strategic forcing activities, and thus the same problems would still exist. As one R&D manager put it: "The problem is that an early venture *is* entrepreneurial; it needs an entrepreneurial type." The problem then is how to "manage" the entrepreneur; how to use this individual optimally.

The suggestion is often made to utilize short-term start-up specialists, thus "professionalizing" the function:

> We must learn to deal better with the traumatic experience of the transition. Senior management must learn to counsel the entrepreneur, to warn him of upcoming problems, of the possibility of having to take it away from him; of how to reintegrate him. Maybe you can keep him for an agglomeration function—putting together a number of small-volume businesses into one venture—or he may go on to manage the entrepreneurial phase of the next venture.

The Psychological Costs of Commitment

Our case studies suggest that entrepreneurship requires deep commitment on the part of the venture manager, not just participation. This then is a major impediment in the efforts to professionalize the function of the entrepreneur. The "participating" type is willing to hand over the reins and to start all over for the corporation. The "committed" type, however, seems to feel differently. For such a person smooth recycling would be impossible. These are the words of one venture manager who was removed:

> Be a "start-up" expert? I don't see that as a viable role for me personally. To be an entrepreneur means a lot of headaches; it means a lot of

work. My average work day is 20 percent higher now than that of the average guy here; it was 100 percent longer when I was the general manager of the new venture. It's a combination of challenge and suffering. You, as the general manager, must set the style for the others.

I do not intend to do that for this company again. Maybe for myself, or for another corporation, perhaps a smaller one, because it was also a tremendous education. But it's also a total investment of the ego. Not everybody can do that. You give up your family. It's risky; you need tremendous confidence in yourself.

True entrepreneurs seem to want to play for keeps, and they may be the only ones who can perform the necessary strategic forcing efforts.

"Coaching": The Casualty of Strategic Neglect

Just as strategic forcing on the part of the venture manager leads to strategically neglecting to build the broad infrastructure of the new-business organization, strategic building on the part of their superiors in the new-venture division of the corporation leads to strategic neglect of "coaching" the entrepreneur.

One possible reason for the lack of coaching is the very style of the entrepreneur: the independent-mindedness of this individual, his or her resistance to receiving advice, and the secrecy of the entrepreneur regarding possible intentions and moves. Another possible reason is the lack of experience on the part of the venture manager's manager. New projects are by definition nonroutine, and upper management does not know *in advance* which organizational problems are only trivial and transient and which ones are going to lead to serious long-run trouble. Coaching at best is corrective rather than guiding.

More importantly, however, the strategic neglect of coaching activities in this entrepreneurial stage of the new venture results from the pressures exerted by the need for fast growth. Aware of the often ambivalent attitudes of corporate management toward unrelated diversification, the upper-level development manager wants to continue the momentum built up by the strategic forcing of the entrepreneurial venture manager.

Upper management in the new-business area is also involved in the organizational championing efforts (see Chapter 5) on behalf of the new venture; here upper management interfaces with top management on behalf of the new venture. In this early stage in the new venture's life, top management will be nervous about their commitment and may require a great deal of reassurance. Thus, strategic building together with organizational championing requires a major time commitment on the part of the upper-level development manager.

As long as the venture managers are meeting their targets and the rapid forced growth is continuing, there is an obvious reluctance to interfere with these entrepreneurs and risk injuring that growth. In effect, the entrepreneurs are being "set up" (inadvertently) for a distressing fall from grace.

Ironically and perversely, the reasons for this appear to be centered on the dedication of the venture manager. This individual's boss is able to observe his or her dedication and commitment. There is an awareness of the efforts and sacrifices made by the new-venture manager, but there may not be adequate compensation to the individual. There certainly won't be equitable compensation if the venture manager has to be removed. Thus the temptation is to procrastinate, to hope that the venture manager will learn or that the problems he or she is having will go away.

Often, however, the problems persist and accumulate because the new-venture manager does not learn to operate within a complex business organization. When corrective action is taken, it is both harsh and belated and usually means the loss of an entrepreneur-in-residence for the corporation.

Conclusion

The major dilemma in the entrepreneurial stage of the new venture is the inherent conflict between forced growth and sound business development. Since top management uses almost as its sole criterion of success for the new venture its ability to show this rapid takeoff, venture managers are encouraged to neglect the development of a durable business structure and sound operating system. In the early stages these vital assets cannot be measured and are likely to be neglected in favor of rapid growth. This is often the undoing of a new venture. Not only will the embryonic business not be able to continue its rate of growth without an organization (functional differentiation, delegation, and the like), but top management, at some point, will change the rules of the game and begin evaluating the managerial skills of the entrepreneur.

Understandably there is both bitterness and waste of personnel associated with these contradictory signals. How to reduce the number of managerial casualties involved in internal corporate venturing without narrowing too much the scope of these efforts is one major challenge for corporate management. How to cope better with the casualties that are unavoidable in high-risk ventures is a second major challenge. A third, more immediate challenge concerns how to consolidate the gains achieved by the entrepreneur, so that his or her efforts were not in vain.

CHAPTER 7

From a One-Product to a Multiline Business

The Organizational Stage

During the early development stages, a great deal of the rapidity and effectiveness of the development takes place because there is a *small group* involved. These stages benefit from the driving forces associated typically with small groups: clear goals, personalized leadership, close physical proximity, unequivocal reinforcement by team members of behavior supporting the attainment of project goals. Team members see each other sacrificing personal goals and facilitating each other's efforts. Enormous productive energies are released and directed toward the needs of the project. If team members are carefully selected and isolated from the mundane "rest of the organization," a "can-do" atmosphere emerges and is sustained by successful completion of milestones as well as by the loyalty arising from doing it "against all odds" and "in spite of" organizational constraints. The Data General case narrated by Kidder in *The Soul of a New Machine*[1] is by now a classic example. Recently, an article in *Business Week*[2] described in a similar vein how IBM's successful development of the personal computer (PC) was achieved by a small, highly motivated group.

Yet, for all its romantic appeal such a period of heroism cannot last. In our study too, we saw that the entrepreneurial stage—the small-group stage—converted the embryonic innovative project into a one-product, self-sustaining business. Strategic forcing was the key to establishing a credible beachhead for the new venture. However, as we also saw, such single-purpose activity often leads to the neglect of continuing new-product development. This may well be fatal if not corrected because it can hold the venture size down to a level that does not meet the minimum size requirements of the corporation, and it can also lead to a failure to maintain the original product's market competitiveness.

Furthermore, the overemphasis on being different, on the need to "shake off the dust crust of the corporation" (as one manager put it), creates a dangerous schism. Useful information, expertise, and experience existing in the corporation's operating system remain untapped by the new venture. We documented how some of this happened at United in the R&D area (see Chapter 6). And it seems to be a general phenomenon. *Time* magazine recently lost $47,000,000 when it abandoned an effort to develop a totally new type of magazine for the cable industry, one that would be custom-tailored to each cable market. According to the *Wall Street Journal* the idea's originators in *Time* magazine's new-publication group failed to undertake any serious consultation with *Time's* own captive cable experts—their Home Box Office (HBO) group.[3]

The final stage of the innovation cycle, the *organizational stage*, should remedy these omissions and help build an appropriate administrative structure for the new venture, including functional specialization and planning capability. At this point the one-product business will develop into a mature multiproduct business which fits in the corporate context. This can be done in two ways. The new business can become a major new department in an existing operating division. This solution is appropriate if the venture can draw on the resources and administrative expertise of the receiving division. Alternatively, the venture may not fit into any existing division and will have to be upgraded to the status of a new freestanding component in the corporate structure.

Unbalanced Administrative Development

The entrepreneurial stage usually leaves the venture with a lopsided administrative development which reflects the biases of the entrepreneurial venture manager. How loose things can become is illustrated in this observation of one executive brought in to improve the administration of a new venture:

> If you look back at it, we have been doing some things which were too much ahead of our needs, and with other things we were too much behind. For instance, we have this tremendous market research library with all kinds of costly subscriptions, but nobody knows what questions to ask that can be answered by the information available. So I am trying to cut those expenses somewhat down. Also, we have developed product line P&L statements, but we haven't gotten the *total* under control: different people will give different estimates of that overall number, so we are focusing on the wrong thing. We have no systematic information on what we have actually sold. We also know that we must clean up the accounts receivable mess on the West Coast because we know that something is going wrong there.

At the beginning of the organizational stage, venture personnel still work in an atmosphere of quickly shifting priorities. Often they are not used to working in the framework of a budget system that becomes increasingly critical because of the larger number of trade-offs required by the growing complexity of a multi-product business. The problem at this stage is not only one of developing a system with rules and regulations, procedures and routines, but also one of teaching and encouraging people to use them. However, this teaching and encouraging process is impeded by the fact that many of the venture participants have been hired from outside the corporation. Opportunistically, many consider their venture participation only as a stepping-stone to an ever-better position in still another corporation.

Venture managers are reluctant to make the kind of trade-offs and compromises that are indigenous to operating organizations. As the venture moves into the organizational stage, they object strenuously to being placed in a position where they must choose among competing interests without any clear maximization. This manager was still being naive when he said:

> I have some underutilized people. One of them would fit well into our new manufacturing function. But if I transfer him, I may find in a month or two that I need him back, and they won't want to part with him. Yet, if I keep him, my labor costs will look too high in the short run. I don't see how one can manage with all these budget changes and switching of priorities.

And the new functional managers still behave as though they

were operating in a entrepreneurial environment rather than being part of an integrated management system. The people in venture management discover that it is difficult to harness their energies. Here is a description of managers in the entrepreneurial stage:

> Too many people are eager to do things for their own sake rather than things that are relevant. Many think they are only working if they alter the information they get and change their assignment so it is "their" project. They want action all the time.

Thus there are two problems in the evolution of functional capabilities beyond the recognition that they are necessary. First, the managers available to lead are used to being in an entrepreneurial environment that rewards ad hoc, spontaneous, and highly individualistic efforts. Secondly, there is little experience with operating in an environment of shared responsibility, teamwork, and carefully worked-through decisions involving multiple (and sometimes contradictory) goals. As one experienced executive said:

> You need the entrepreneurial phase, and then you must develop functional capabilities. The problem is that there is a strong tendency toward continued "entrepreneurship" because people believe that if we develop something new, then somebody will buy it; they cannot recognize that at some point you must start pointing your technology. As an organization grows, there is a dominating need for developing functional capabilities, but then you have got to control what these functions are going to do: you need to give them direction, to harness this tremendous amount of latent energy. At some point, you need to reassert the management control of the business so that the functions do something *profitable*, and not just "something."

It is also necessary to teach the functional managerial people to direct their contribution more broadly, in the light of the objectives of the overall venture rather than in narrow functional terms, and to make them feel secure enough that they are willing to recognize that there may be problems that require more integrated approaches:

> It takes time. Many of these opportunists—what we call "gun slingers" around here—leave, and only then can the system settle down. Also, you must superimpose a sense of teamwork and a business structure. Only when you are able to develop a sense of continuity will people recognize that problems exist.

110

In short, at this late stage of development, when innovation must gradually give way to institutionalization, some of the more typical managerial problems begin to assert themselves in full force. As one of the authors has discussed elsewhere,[4] the various functional groups of the venture are now being measured in terms of their own internal goals, efficiencies, and routines, which is almost exactly the opposite of the small group conditions described above. A reluctance to being flexible sets in. The members of each group seek to avoid deferring and compromising, because they fear that their short-run performance will be hurt. Also, if the venture experiences difficulties in marketing or production, great pressure from top management (now fully aware of the outsiders) to reach objectives will cause various groups to tighten up, to try to prove that other departments are at fault. More importantly, perhaps, such pressure from top management tends to reduce the new-venture's managerial team's capabilities of dealing with previously unrecognized problems in the field, its potential for increasing efficiency, and its ability to implement advantageous product modifications. All of these, of course, require evolving a real business structure.

Evolving an Administrative Framework

At the entrepreneurial stage, the structure is simple, direct, and often very effective. It is not much different from the traditional small business in which everything revolves around and is integrated through the owner-manager. Given the incentives of ownership (or venture identification and commitment), intense personal efforts serve to coordinate the various parts and guarantee reasonable consistency between what is being done in marketing, R&D, and manufacturing. Furthermore, insofar as the total professional/managerial group is reasonably small, the parts are held together by the opportunity for direct, easy contact and a sense of membership in a fast-moving, potentially very rewarding enterprise.

But these experiences and this small-group culture is a deterrent to the evolution of a total new business. The latter presumes multiple decision makers, a more sophisticated structure than exists at the level of the informal small group, a true administrative framework, and management systems.

111

There has been overdependence on the energies and creativity of the entrepreneur–project champion. Eventually, organizational pressures for the "routinization of charisma"[5] exert themselves, making the entrepreneur flounder. This individual has been too busy, too absorbed and involved in one product. Overconcentration and what we have called "strategic neglect" have impoverished the development effort. It turns out to be more difficult than expected to replicate the initial success with the new product.

Ironically, as we have already observed, a major problem of new-venture development is new-product development.

> Our core product was very successful but its successor was neglected. It was very late in development. Engineering didn't have tight requirements placed upon it, and the marketing program was being changed all the time without having to justify why its initial plans had been set up a certain way. Furthermore, we haven't learned to coordinate hardware and software. At the inception they were both clearly coordinated but 18 months down the line, when the hardware developed moved to engineering and production, they no longer fitted together.

Collaboration has now become more important but there aren't the administrative mechanisms to facilitate and impose this discipline. An administrative framework for a new business presumes more dispersed decision-making. Everything no longer flows through the hands and mind of the entrepreneur. In practice this means that, for example, R&D and marketing people have to learn to negotiate compromises on product specifications, and manufacturing has to learn to negotiate with a new purchasing group on whether a readily available standard component might be a reasonable substitute for a much more expensive vendor's custom line.

In the established operating divisions, these lateral relations and day-to-day agreements are facilitated by several factors which the new organization doesn't yet enjoy:

1. A common culture which has developed over a period of years, shared by most participants and communicated by a variety of cues and symbols, indoctrination, and a common reward system.

> In our division we always use outside vendors for noncritical parts and materials with limited usage and high instability in demands. We never use outside vendors for regularly used supplies with predictable demand functions. But those guys in that new venture can't decide whether to "make or buy" anything and everything.

2. Reasonably established jurisdictional lines and status and power differentials have evolved so that resolving a problem between two functions doesn't appear to threaten established jurisdictions.

> In contrast to the operating divisions, our managers [in a new venture] are reluctant to compromise or to concede any issue to their counterparts in another function for fear it will either imply they are too weak or shift the balance of power or set a dangerous precedent in which the other department can dominate them.

3. Size and financial strength permits business managers to deal as equals with specialist functional groups. Reporting directly to the product managers are assistants or staff with the ability and training to penetrate functional groups and evaluate their recommendations and requirements.

> In a new venture there are few problems between the product managers and functional managers as long as the former are simply telling the latter *what* to do. If they intend to also tell them *how* to do things the product managers better have some specialists that report directly to them or they will get "snowed" every time by the functions.

Marketing Versus R&D in Product Planning

There is also a continuing struggle between marketing and R&D. Marketing people complain:

> We still don't get involved at the inception of new-product planning. It is the technology area that determines what we sell.

And for their part, the R&D people still complain that marketing people can't seem to provide clear guidelines. In the words of the R&D manager of a venture:

> Marketing should provide us with what I call "essential characteristics of new products," for instance, that it is necessary to have a 1-minute rather than a 1-hour fiber test. Marketing actually provides product management with complaints rather than fundamental guidelines: they respond to R&D, then they criticize.
>
> It's a function of the personnel involved. We need scientists in marketing; we need much more interdisciplinary training. I have already brought in two Ph.D.'s as product managers in marketing, but take another guy like X. who is in marketing research—he knows a lot of information but cannot evaluate it.

113

From the perspective of the marketing people, the problem is not one of reacting versus guiding. In fact, the marketing people often argue that marketing ultimately has the power to define in which areas new products will be developed and what the technology requirements are:

> Actually, marketing has an edge, because I can define the scope of the business. I can say it won't work; I can skew the numbers. So marketing can have an influence over what products we are going to work on. What marketing does not have an influence over are what the features of the new product will be.

From marketing's perspective, the problem is to control the work that takes place within the directions and boundaries set by them:

> The problem is to keep controlling them. They take your money, but then the "needs of science" become paramount. So we are now working on some schemes to put our foot down without hurting people.

These new-product development problems are often not recognized at the corporate level. This may be the consequence of failing to distinguish between new ideas and new products. The former is indeed no problem at all because, as one of the business managers pointed out:

> If we get in the x market we will be flooded with inventors knocking at our door. Because we have what the inventor does not have: (1) the capability for market penetration, and (2) at least so they think, money. It is not difficult to get outside ideas for new development.

Even in the light of repeated new-product failures in these growing ventures, there seems to be a pervasive feeling that there is no need to worry about "add-on" products since "there are always plenty of new ideas." Corporate management may thus underestimate the gap between an idea and a salable product.

In the relation between R&D and marketing, there is substantial tension in a fluid technology as to who is guiding whom, who sets the parameters and who responds. The initiative usually goes to those with the stronger technological training since the nontechnical people find it difficult, as we have seen, to provide comparable hard data and to define their needs in explicit, objective terms.

But we observed one highly successful marketing manager in the

114

organizational stage who was able to initiate to and get responsiveness from his technical colleagues. He was able to make explicit:

- What the marketplace required in terms of product performance
- Therefore, what problems needed to be solved by the technical people
- What was "in it" for the R&D people, their stake in this problem solving
- What was "in it" for manufacturing and other operations groups to justify their making certain concessions

The Growing Importance of Manufacturing

Among the functions, previously neglected, that need institutionalizing is obviously manufacturing. Many corporations undertaking new ventures establish a special start-up facility which allows diverse fabrication and production requirements to be met. At some point, however, the new enterprise needs its own facilities and associated managerial skills.

There is one difficult trade-off here. Developing in-house manufacturing may close off alternative technologies too early. Continued use of the special start-up facilities and contracting out allows the enterprise to maintain many options with respect to the kind of technology to utilize for a given product configuration. The absence of a significant fixed investment may encourage more innovative product development. Other studies suggest that product innovation is injured by excessive emphasis on incremental process improvements once the major parameters of the product become fixed.[6]

On the other hand, reliance on outsiders obviously injures the ability of the business to control and develop its manufacturing capabilities.

The Changing Relation to Corporate R&D

As the business grows it must cut the "umbilical cord" to the corporate R&D organization. It must have the talent and be given the budget and goal of generating relevant new technologies. The ideal is a

115

delicate balance between overdependence on the corporate staff (perhaps through starving the new business's function) and outright rejection of the resources contained in the centralized function.

The Need for Strategic Management

Just as one person (the entrepreneur) can no longer carry all the elements in his or her head, make all trade-offs, and perform all coordination, he or she can no longer be the only person responsible for strategy formulation. Strategy must grow out of the knowledge of a number of people with diverse experiences and responsibilities. Good strategic planning grows out of the legitimate trade-offs between product and functional considerations. Over time, as the new business adds products and services and institutionalized functional competency, these trade-offs become more complex and more necessary. This is in sharp contrast to one person weighing and balancing alternative criteria.

The need for a systematic approach to strategy making increases dramatically as a result of successful strategic building in the entrepreneurial stage. In a medical equipment venture, for instance, United was eventually competing in four different business areas. In each of these areas, strong competitors (both small and large ones) existed. It became quite clear that, in order to survive in each of these areas, it was necessary for United to build a strategic management capability into the venture organization.

Relations with Corporate Management

Two problems seem to recur. Insofar as the new business represents a different type of business from those represented in existing operating divisions, there is a sense of estrangement. As the head of one new and growing venture described this:

> I have been spending more time with the corporate head of our new-venture and R&D activities. He tells me, "You guys are so different, the corporation doesn't understand you. You must involve us more in the running of the business."

116

Of course, more involvement of corporate management can be threatening given the autonomy that has nourished the venture to date. Undoubtedly there is the recognition that "coming of age" means accepting a number of encumbering rules, procedures, and norms which may not be consistent with the culture that has evolved in the new venture.

The other source of anxiety is whether the venture can attain enough stature (annual revenues) to justify membership in the corporate operating community. Again, the head of a new venture states:

> The corporation's interest in us is conditional on us becoming big enough ($50 to $100 million in annual sales). If we stay small, then the corporation and us have little to offer each other. We could not justify the attention of the management committee [that oversees the operating divisions] and the use of other management time. Just as important, the corporation doesn't know how to run a small business.

In a sense the new business receives conflicting signals, at least at United, as it reaches the organizational stage. There are still lots of cues suggesting that forced and thereby fast growth is expected—and rewarded. At the same time the corporation appears to be saying, "adopt and conform to the norms and values and procedures of the larger organization."[7]

The conflict arises when the culture of the larger organization appears antithetical to fast growth. For example, the greater formality, the greater number of meetings, clearances, and procedures—all appear time- and resource-consuming and a detraction from the hectic "growth at any price" philosophy of the earlier stages. And, of course, they are meant to be so. The larger organization is seeking to socialize the new unit so it will fit and be consistent with the other divisions. Standardization and conformity not only "look right," they facilitate the operation of numerous management systems, for example, personnel, interdivisional relationships, budget making, and accounting.

This will be a period when there may well be a shake-out of those too individualistic entrepreneurial types who can't tolerate systems and structure and won't be tamed. They are the ones who say, "No way can you spend time in meetings and really keep up that hard running."

The sharp contrast between executives in operations and new ventures in both organizational culture and orientation is illustrated in the following observations of a United manager:

> In the division, the decisions are always "team" decisions. Now that's a safer environment because once you have gone through the screening process that brings you to a certain position where you have limited responsibility, you are never going to be able to do anything dramatically bad, but by the same token you also cannot do anything dramatically good in a personalized sense. To create our new business United was forced to go outside to hire people. Now these tend to be opportunistic people who are often more interested in making a name for themselves, so that they can jump to a next and even better position. So they tend to push the things in their area that they can put on their resume, specific things that they have accomplished, but which in the overall framework of the new business may not have been the best things. We have got quite a few of these "hot shot" types.

And from a manager who had been hired from outside United:

> Here, we all are new. We are "gunfighters," problem solvers, focusing on the short term. As we grow larger, more decisions must be filtered through the corporate system. But so far, everybody acts independently; *nobody monitors me now*, and I like that. In a way we are all entrepreneurs here. If we grow and become more structured, many of us may leave.

Controls

Control systems that work in the operating components are often inadequate for the ambiguous and quickly changing environment of the innovating system. The assumption underlying control in the large, complex, operational components is that everybody needs to know all the time what is going on. Hence, there is constant reporting and monitoring of the business activities.

New ventures, in contrast, often need to protect themselves from close scrutiny. This "hiding" is needed to get time to build up credibility with upper management. Because of the great variations in activity from period to period in the entrepreneurial stage, the new-venture management is afraid of alarming corporate management when there are serious problems, or even more threatening, to raise corporate management's expectations too high too soon in periods of fast growth.

The new venture also needs to avoid possible encroachments by operating subdivisions that are asserting jurisdictional authority and to avoid tempting its operations side to absorb an attractive new activity.

New-venture management also seeks to resist corporate regulations, to "cut corners" in regard to standard operating procedures. Not to do so might in fact jeopardize the survival chances of the venture:

> One factor in the success of a new venture was that the venture manager decided to start selling a product from a certain location, even though it was against company regulations.

Reward Systems

Corporate regulations regarding salary levels were also an obstacle to acquiring key people:

> United cannot afford to buy people; they have all these regulations and strict salary scales. So you will go to the administration and say we need these two guys and they want $80,000, and they will say "wait a minute, how long have they been working, what was their previous salary, what level are they going to work at in United?" And they will look at some charts, get their calculators out, and say "we cannot do it," and so you don't get the people you need. Thus United did not get any of the technical people from Alpha. Yet, two or three people there had all the knowledge of the technological problems and all the secrets, and so we did not get any of that.

The reward system at United did not fit the needs of new ventures. Typically, the corporation attached great weight to the volume of dollars managed as an indicator of managerial responsibility. This fits the operating system well but fails to reward adequately the efforts of the new-development people, for whom level of responsibility is more related to problem identification and creative solution.

> You must compare what the outside entrepreneur can have in terms of incentives and freedoms with what a corporation like United can give. The outside entrepreneur can get equity participation, capital gains, particular ways of financing. He has short lines of communication, little overhead, and can engage in courses of action that are "not done by United," and so forth. The only advantage for the inside entrepreneur is

119

Table 7-1

Systematic Differences Between the Operating System and New Ventures

Operating System	New Ventures
Modest amount of uncertainty	Major unknowns, major changes in parameters occur "overnight"
Emphasis on meticulous planning, incremental balanced growth, sequential and systematic decision making, and assumed relative stability	Emphasis on opportunistic risk taking, unbalanced growth, sudden bursts of activity—"forcing" and instability
Long experience with lateral relations, negotiating between "product" and "functional" objectives and standards	Used to autonomous operations, wary that trade-offs will reduce authority or sphere of influence
Emphasis on planning; stable growth objectives	Emphasis on expedient, real-time adjustment, entrepreneurship; radical newness
Realistic behavioral understanding of how one job fits with others	Unusual to think of job interfaces
Corporate and rule-oriented, formalized	Individualistic, unconstrained
Employee values homogeneous; most have long service in the same organization	Employees heterogeneous, drawn from diverse sources

the stable paycheck, and one can wonder whether that is an incentive at all for the real entrepreneur. . . . So that's a real problem. I think that we will need some dispensation from United's policies if we want to develop this entrepreneurial climate. We should find a way of giving these people "decorations."

Regrettably, the cultural experiences of managers in new ventures do not prepare them for becoming part of the institutionalized family. They must unlearn as much as they must learn, and habitual patterns of thought and action are not changed that easily. Table 7-1 summarizes some of the differences among these two cultures that we have observed.

Conclusion

In this chapter, we have discussed the organizational stage of a new venture. During this stage, corporate organizational reality catches up with the new venture's turbulent past. Many deficiencies resulting from the entrepreneurial way of doing things must be remedied to assure the continued viability of the venture and to integrate it into the corporate structure. This is a period of high anxiety for the venture personnel. Not surprisingly, there are unusually high turnover and lots of concerns about relative position and influence as the administrative framework becomes streamlined in the corporate mold.

If anything, this stage creates a heightened awareness of the fundamental paradox involved in internal corporate venturing: the chaos associated with autonomous strategic behavior on the part of nontypical participants is necessary to get something going; but eventually administrative discipline must be imposed in order for the corporation to take advantage of the new strategic thrust that has been launched by its entrepreneurs. A major challenge for corporate management is then how to create an internal environment for dealing with this fundamental paradox. At United, the development process that we have described took place in the context of the new-venture division (NVD), the establishment of which was supposed to provide an adequate response to the challenge. In Chapter 8, we shall examine further to what extent the NVD does, indeed, serve this purpose well.

CHAPTER 8

The New-Venture Division
in the Corporate Context

The previous chapters have sought to summarize our findings concerning the major stages new businesses pass through as they are initiated and evolve in a large, diversified corporation. We now wish to focus a bit more on the impact of this intricate process on top management's activity and perceptions as they try to structure an internal environment for internal corporate venturing (ICV).

In reading what has been said about major corporations and their innovative capabilities, one gets the impression that there is almost a love-hate relationship. Particularly in this period of great economic uncertainty, high rates of product obsolescence, and extraordinary competitive pressures, few corporate leaders would admit to being anti-innovation. Yet many would wonder whether a relatively "free-wheeling" culture can coexist under the same corporate skin with traditional, proceduralized business. In our study we have chosen a somewhat "most difficult" condition in which the corporation is seeking to innovate in fields that are unfamiliar and removed from its established product lines.

Is There an Anti-innovation Bias in the Large Corporation?

There certainly are outstanding examples of major innovations being born in large corporations. American Telephone and Telegraph (AT&T) bred the transistor, and large corporate R&D departments have a rich lode of new technologies and new products to their credit. Nevertheless, observers and researchers note the presence of a number of counterinnovation forces in the large corporation. The American steel and auto industries have been well-publicized whipping boys in this regard.

For two or three decades the U.S. auto industry appeared to resist technological changes (e.g., fuel injection or new, efficient engines), preferring instead to invest in safer manufacturing processes and cosmetic design changes.[1] Change was forced upon U.S. auto manufacturers by competition from overseas. Worse yet, the steel industry appeared to resist even process changes (such as continuous processing and the basic oxygen furnace) which had become proven cost-efficient technologies in Japan and in Europe.

Students of organization have found a number of bases for conservatism which go beyond subjective charges of mismanagement or sloth born of monopoly power. The managerial styles required by well-routinized operations are very different from the approaches that seem to work for managing innovation. Some years ago Williamson wrote: "[A] division of effort between the new product innovation process on the one hand, and the management of proven resources on the other may well be efficient."[2] Whenever observers have looked systematically at both administrative styles and organization structure in routinized as compared with change-oriented technologies, they have noted substantial differences.

The pressures of corporate long-range planning systems and shorter-range control systems induce an emphasis on carefully planned improvements and stable growth. These are not compatible with highly volatile, unpredictable innovations. Rather, they encourage incremental change in both products and processes. Large organizations appear to have as goals minimal fluctuation, stability, and predictability.

Managers who flourish in such environments are not likely to be "high rollers," looking for a big breakthrough, but rather solid "corporate citizens." Senior managers have grown used to a system in which there are few clear-cut individual decisions. Most important decisions within the operating divisions are team decisions.

Of course, operating divisions can also have their own R&D units dedicated to developing related new products and services. Such divisional efforts confront a number of challenges. It is difficult to amass and justify a "critical mass" of first-rate researchers and well-equipped laboratories except at the corporate-wide level. More significantly, such divisional efforts tend to show erratic support for projects generated by their R&D groups that are outside their mainstream divisional strategies, but are potentially quite important for corporate development. In boom times, when existing products are doing very well, new projects are often regarded as "misfits" and ignored. In economic downturns, even dubious projects may be embraced, thus insuring a high failure rate. Extreme cyclicality is of course inconsistent with the sustained, persevering support that is essential for significant breakthroughs that become economically successful.

An Organizational Innovation: New-Venture Divisions to Create New Business

It thus seems very reasonable to expect that corporations would seek to create a parallel—separate but equal?—system that was more consistent with the needs of new, high-growth, high-risk, unstable products and technologies. Many years before, this had been the objective of the separate corporate R&D laboratory. But the institutionalization of a more professional (even academic, "adhocratic") organization assumed that once the new discovery was proven it could be transplanted to an existing division where it would flourish in the established context of corporate business operations.

However, radically new products have no obvious locations into which they can be transplanted. Furthermore, sophisticated managers have come to recognize that there is much more to developing a radically new product and technology than proving the concept in the laboratory. New, relatively unproven activities require a great deal of mutual give and take, the ability to cope with a number of unanticipated crises (and opportunities), a management that may delegate less (and be intimately involved in detailed day-to-day decision-making), and an absence of written procedures. Entrepreneurially inclined managers, looking for large "wins" and accordingly willing to take large risks, will most likely be self-selected.

In retrospect, it seems quite logical that an organizational innovation, the new-venture division (NVD), would be created. NVDs decouple the new ventures from the established sphere of business operations and seek to move their development to a place of some self-sufficiency. The NVD provides an internal-to-the-corporation environment in which new business opportunities can be explored, incubated, turned into projects, and provided with the opportunity to demonstrate economic viability. At that point they should presumably be more readily able to be integrated into existing divisions or to be established as new operating divisions of the corporation.[3]

That is the theory: two structures and associated cultures; one for established, reasonably routinized technologies, and one for just-born and about-to-be-born new products and technologies. However, of course, organizations can't be neatly divided into impermeably bounded units. The fact that there are a common top management and certain overall corporate goals and the need for certain interchanges between the new ventures and the older established business divisions leads inevitably to some clashes. In Chapter 7 we discussed some of the systematic differences between the culture of the established division and that of the evolving new ventures. Additional indirect but convincing evidence of the incongruities and inconsistencies between the "two cultures" is reflected in the precarious position of NVDs in the firm and the frequency with which they are reorganized or disbanded.[4]

The NVD–Operating Divisions Interface

We have just described the logic of creating a separate structure to encourage a sphere of substantial innovation both removed from and buffered from the routines, values, and culture of a firm's established operating divisions. But as with every other kind of boundary or interface in real-life organizations, the boundary between new-venture and operation divisions is hardly impenetrable. In fact, it is desirable that a number of exchanges and agreements take place across the boundary. Given the major differences in orientation and even managerial instincts, one would not expect these to be consistently harmonious or easy to manage.

Strategic Conflicts of Interest

At the divisional level, *domain* and *synergy* issues emerge whenever the new-business activities have the potential to overlap with the activities of the division. Struggles to protect one's domain and discussions about the positive and/or negative synergy consequences almost unavoidably occur. For instance, in one case in our study a major issue concerned the relative advantage of selling large volumes of new fiber at a low profit margin per unit of volume, versus selling relatively small quantities of "components" to new customers further down the industrial chain at relatively high profit margins. In another case, a division expressed concerns about possible negative synergy resulting from the new venture's sales force calling on its customers with a very different selling approach.

The domain and synergy issues become especially difficult in those cases where the master strategy for the new area of business leads to attempts to take projects arising in other divisions of the corporation and agglomerate them under the venture's administrative umbrella (we have termed this "strategic building"). A critical skill in maintaining viability for a venture caught in the web of corporate strategic interests was therefore the ability of the NVD management to stay ahead of the game. Thus, in the case of the new fibers mentioned above, a high-level manager in the NVD was quick to suggest the creation of a "steering committee" in which all interests were to be represented, including those of the corporate operating divisions. This manager thus sought to prevent the venture from being smothered by the powerful division from which the fibers were to be obtained. In the words of the venture manager:

> The manager initiated the "steering committee" because he wanted the support from other people in the corporation. He got the support of the vice-chairman of the board, who wrote a letter to all presidents and vice-presidents of the divisions involved. All possible conflicts are settled in the committee. It's a very practical tool, excellent for conflict resolution. As a result, we have gotten all the support we want.

In the case of a venture that manufactured medical equipment, the venture management people not only created a committee but also astutely handled the narrow divisional interests in one-on-one relationships. The manager involved in this described it as follows:

> In the case of the "blood bank" project, that project existed in the Cryogenics division. I used the Jet Propulsion Laboratory, my contacts

there, as a carrot. The Cryogenics division is interested in freezers as commercial products, not as medical products. The device uses patents owned by CIT [California Institute of Technology] and NASA, and there are some attractive aspects in the development of new freezing equipment. So I told the Cryogenics division guys, "Let me handle the medical equipment, it's only about 15 percent of the total volume. And you guys just grab the pull-out." It was part business, part friendship here. In part, it was also horse-trading.

In short, jurisdictional conflicts will have to be worked through. At times, a new venture will want to gain control over a critical product that is now the property of an operating division. Astute negotiating will be required, even "horse-trading" to provide the giver with some relevant compensation. It would be naive to assume that these exchanges take place solely in the context of what would maximize the well-being of the total corporation.

Administrative Conflicts

Quite aside from the important strategic issues of synergy and domain, even simple work flow issues get hung up at the border between NVD and operating divisions due to administrative factors. Through its emphasis on action plans and lateral sign-offs, the corporate *management system* facilitates the functioning of the complex work flows in the operating divisions and enhances the incremental innovation processes in that part of the corporation. At the same time, such a management system hinders the functioning of the NVD. Perhaps most importantly, the management system impedes the flow of ideas across internal organizational boundaries. Various participants in our study noted the existence of isolated pockets of relevant capabilities in various parts of the corporation. They pointed to the need to create cross-communication between these, but as one of them observed:

> The management system makes cross-communication very difficult. For instance, I can call up contacts in other parts of the corporation and pick their brains. But I cannot say, "I have this idea and you have this equipment, would you do three samples for me?" The other person will say he cannot do it because his time is already allotted in the action plans, and if he does this, it might have a negative impact on his performance appraisal.

127

This situation tends to force someone to go through his or her superior to get something done in another part of the corporation. But these tactics could reduce the willingness of the higher-up person to actually do what has been requested. Said one scientist:

> If I wanted to explore something in the dermatology area, I would have to make contact in the other parts of the corporation. But I must go to my boss first. Now he may think, "Pete is working on something," and you know that sooner or later he is going to ask you about it. So you hesitate to try to find out. Half-baked ideas need to be checked out, but you don't want to talk it through with somebody who has an impact on your evaluation. So, often you will drop something before you have checked it out, or you must make a substantial effort to defend yourself when your idea is challenged. It's stifling.

Furthermore, the assumption underlying the management system in the large, highly structured divisions is that everybody needs to know all the time what everybody else is doing. Hence, there is constant reporting and monitoring of the divisions' activities. New ventures, in contrast, need at times to protect themselves from close scrutiny. This is necessary to avoid "roadblocks" that people in operating divisions might put up if a potential problem of conflict of domain existed, or to avoid awakening an operating division's desire to absorb the venture prematurely.

Not surprisingly, perhaps, the way the operating division people perceive the new venture affects their collaboration with the NVD. To the extent that the new venture is viewed as exciting and has shown some initial success, operating division people find it gratifying to help out the other group and are less likely to refer to their own action plans and limited time. A manager of a successful new venture described his experience.

> We are somewhat glamorous. Divisional people have been a tremendous help; they act as my consultants. For formal projects we pay, but for an effort of 2 or 3 days, even a week, we don't have to. This corporation has all the skills. You must find the people, develop bonds. I guess that the key to the whole thing is that what we are doing sounds more challenging than what they are doing, so they are glad to be part of the action.

Another interface problem is related to *personnel transfers*. As noted earlier, the NVD tends to attract and select different types of people than the operating system. Basically, one finds two kinds of people in the NVD: the highly able entrepreneurial ones, and those with somewhat limited ability to perform in the complex matrix structure of the operating system who have been put in the NVD to fill vacant slots. Both types find it very difficult to be reabsorbed by the operating system when a project folds. Conversely, it is difficult to get people who feel at ease in the operating system to transfer to the NVD. Such people often view the NVD as "wasting resources and just fooling around" and/or perceive it as a place where it is difficult to "see the results of your work" on a regular basis. One high-level divisional R&D manager explained this problem in relationship to the corporate R&D department:

> Corporate R&D has high standards, but the work there may be perceived as a little less meaningful. People like to see the results of their work, and our people see the results more often.

This perception is even stronger with respect to the divisional business people. In the words of one such business person, who was perhaps somewhat disgruntled: "A really competent guy will not want to take all these risks, he will seek his opportunity elsewhere!" Figure 8-1 summarizes the discussion of the problems in the NVD-operating division interface.

The Interface with Corporate Management

By definition, new ventures are volatile; they don't have the predictable performance from reporting period to reporting period expected of operating divisions. The very existence of the NVD form is partially an effort to shield these infant businesses from the close scrutiny of senior management. Seasoned NVD managers know that is partially myth, but they still believe that it is worth trying to decrease their visibility. When early results are very good, NVD managers worry that corporate's expectations for the future and for extrapolated performance improvements will become unrealistic. In contrast, when short-term results are unfavorable these same managers anticipate close scrutiny, which can inhibit needed flexibility. Poor performance can also lead to decreased support that can make turnarounds more difficult, if not impossible, and thus lead to the creation of a self-confirming prophecy. Inevitably there is ambiguity in the concept of a NVD providing freedom from normal corporate constraints

Figure 8–1

The NVD–Operating System Interface (*From "Managing the New Venture Division: Research Findings and Implications for Strategic Management" by R. A. Burgelman*, Strategic Management Journal, *6(1), January–March 1985. Copyright 1985 by John Wiley & Sons, Ltd. Reprinted by permission of John Wiley & Sons, Ltd.*)

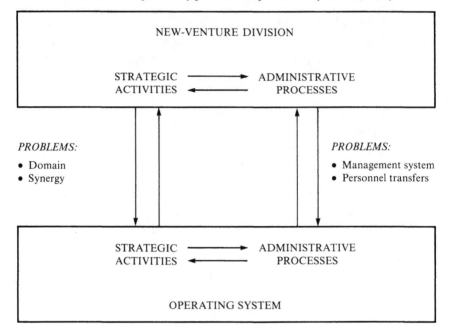

and reporting. As in the old saw, the typical senior corporate manager wants to encourage the breeding of wild ducks but wants to produce those that can quickly learn to fly in formation. Not surprisingly, the ambiguity inherent in the NVD arrangement entails additional friction.

Administrative Friction

Corporate rules and regulations are often viewed as constraints to be circumvented by the NVD participants. Following the rules could, in fact, jeopardize the survival chances of a venture in the early stages of development. In one such case, as we noted earlier, an entrepreneurial manager decided that it was necessary to start selling a product from a certain location, even though it was against company regulations. The same person had started to hire salespeople, even though the project had not yet become an official venture. In other instances, such regulations could not be circumvented and became serious obstacles.

Reward and Measurement Issues

These issues are also a major source of friction. The compensation of the venture managers becomes a serious problem in many instances. These are expected to be highly entrepreneurial, risk-taking executives who bear a heavy burden of work and run a significant risk of injuring the progress of their careers, in case the venture fails. Under the "normal" management salary administration program, their salaries may bear no relationship to what is expected of them.

Venture managers' requests for generous compensation and recognition can influence decision-making adversely. We have already noted that venture managers are driven to force rapid growth, often at the expense of well-rounded management development. At a much earlier stage, ambitious would-be venture managers may become strong champions of a new business idea because it holds out some promise of bringing them great rewards. The "carrot," when very large, may encourage impetuous decisions and opportunism in selecting vehicles to ride toward the goal of rapid advancement. Thus top management unwittingly may seduce managers into making suboptimal decisions.

The problems of a new-venture activity in its relationship to top management represent a common but often ignored subject in management. Management often provides cues or signals that *appear* to be unambiguous. For example, the signals say that managers who meet their profit goals will be the most highly rewarded, or that customer service is paramount.

Rarely, however, are these as one-sided as the naive statement suggests; more hidden messages or caveats are usually present. The reasons for these less overtly stated qualifications or contrary objectives is that some things are less easy to talk about or even a little embarrassing. An organization may not want to state that seniority, for example, as well as "bottom line" performance may have to play a role in promotion. Of course, new ventures are to be treated separately from the more established operations of the corporation (since top management accepts the facts of life—that ventures are high-risk, volatile operations). But while they are treated as unique and given special "soft" handling, they are not totally out of the culture and the corporation seeks to keep their behavior within quite narrow but often unstated limits.

In fact, given the high risk and uncertainty surrounding the cost of innovations and the fears concerning their long-run profitability, excessive attention may be paid to symbolic signs of health or illness in the new venture to reassure higher-level corporate management. While mouthing the standard line that everyone knows it may take x number of years to attain real profitability, senior management may need constant reassuring that the whole thing is really working by seeing some kind of exponential sales growth.

Strategic Management Friction

The establishment of the NVD is often not based on a clear corporate venturing strategy. This has been noted by other students of the venture divisions approach, who observed dramatic changes in the status of such divisions as a result of erratic changes in corporate strategy.[4] Our study reveals a similar situation. New-venture activity was perceived by some of the participants as top management's "insurance"[5] against mainstream business going bad. As one middle-level manager pointed out:

> They are going into new areas because they are not sure that we will be able to stay in the current mainstream businesses. That is also the reason why the time of maturity of a new venture is never right. If current businesses go O.K. then it is always too early, but when current business is not going too well, then we will just jump into anything!

The *lack of a corporate strategy* for diversification, combined with the possibilities in the NVD to avoid the checks and balances existing in the divisions, creates the impression of a "blank check" for strategic behavior in the NVD. But organizations don't write blank checks. There are fields that represent acceptable extensions of existing product lines and those that are unacceptable. The latter may represent new products that are too risky in some way or inconsistent with the *image* of the company maintained by top management. In our study, for instance, it became clear that venture management assumed that top management would let them move into the medical arena with diagnostic but not therapeutic materials or devices. In an environmental systems venture, NVD management was unwilling to let the venture manager sell a certain type of equipment because they feared that it might taint the corporate image if the equipment turned out to be inadequate, and thus might trigger strong top management reaction. These concerns become more pronounced as the venture grows larger and top management becomes more aware of what precisely the venture manager has been doing. As one manager put it in the case of the medical equipment venture:

> You would think that the corporation would have worried a lot about the selling of reagents, and so on. Well, they do now! Corporate management follows things more closely now because Dr. S. [the venture manager] drew a lot of attention.

Also the new-venture activities tend to create pressures for a *rate of strategic change* that eventually is impossible for the company to sustain both for strategic reasons and because of financial resource constraints. As a result, consolidation efforts are imposed by top management that do not necessarily reflect an improved strategic vision. This happened in our study, after the company had allowed the NVD to pursue new businesses for about 7 years. In the words of one high-level manager:

> To be frank, I don't feel corporate management has a clear idea. Recently, we had a meeting with the management committee, and there are now new directives. In fact, I had to write these myself, and they then disagreed with some of it and it was changed. Basically, it de-emphasizes diversification for the moment. The emphasis is on consolidation, with the recognition that diversification will be important in the future. The point is that we will not continue in four or five different areas any more.

Figure 8–2 summarizes the discussion of the problems in the corporate level–NVD interface.

The Uses and Abuses of the New-Venture Division

In this chapter, we have looked at strategic and administrative problems associated with the NVD, an organizational innovation geared toward facilitating new-business development in established firms. Whereas some companies, like 3M, Owens-Illinois, and DuPont, have reported successful experiences with their NVDs, more system-

133

Figure 8–2
The NVD–Corporate Level Interface (*From "Managing the New Venture Division: Research Findings and Implications for Strategic Management" by R. A. Burgelman*, Strategic Management Journal, *6(1), January–March 1985. Copyright 1985 by John Wiley & Sons, Ltd. Reprinted by Permission of John Wiley and Sons, Ltd.*)

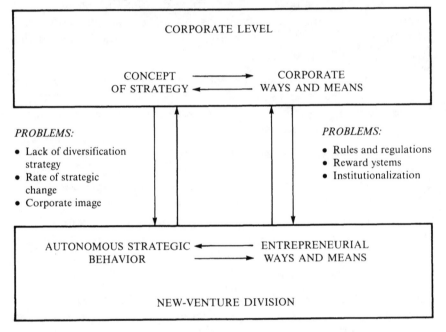

atic research has found the position of the NVD to be precarious in many other firms.

Our study confirms that the NVD is not a panacea for facilitating corporate innovation. It suggests that, perhaps, top management has sometimes allowed the NVD to become the dumping ground for "misfit" and "orphan" projects of the operating divisions. Our study provides evidence that, even when created more deliberately as a vehicle for facilitating new-venture development, the NVD usually has not been guided by a well-thought-out corporate strategy.

Does the NVD Have a Future?

Like most oraganizational innovations, the NVD solves some problems while creating new and often unanticipated ones. This, of course, does not necessarily mean that the NVD design cannot work. It only means that top management should learn from experience. This, in turn, means that a better understanding might be gained of the types of new-business project for which the NVD is a suitable organizational vehicle, and of the additional strategic and administrative measures that top management must consider if it wants to create the conditions under which the NVD can be effective. Chapters 10 and 11 will examine closely the implications of what can be learned from the cumulative corporate experiences associated with NVDs up to the present, and we will propose some recommendations that may serve as a future guide to NVD design in many established firms. But first we would like to propose a conceptual framework that will allow us to depict the complete organizational process involved in ICV.

CHAPTER 9

An Overview of Internal Corporate Venturing

Implementing a Process for Innovation

We have sought to look at new-product development and corporate innovation under highly demanding conditions: the creation of new ventures for products that depart radically from a company's mainstream business sphere. Such a challenge should highlight the managerial requirements for introducing significant product change because the ongoing routines of operations in production and marketing provide little guidance, and the risks of failure (both to careers and as reflected in the P&L statement) are great.

American enterprise is being encouraged to give higher priority to innovation, and it becomes important to know the "way" as well as to have the "will." There is a need for exploration of the actual organizational process by which research ideas and concepts are transmuted into usable, profitable goods and services. There is always the temptation to avoid looking at the details of how innovation gets accomplished in the desire to find the right answer. Improved tax incentives for R&D and better training in "creativity" suggest some of the more typical "solutions" to the innovation problem. In contrast to providing a solution, we have explored the everyday managerial actions, activities, and procedures that facilitate or inhibit the evolution of new products. Furthermore, we have sought to examine these in the actual sequence in which they occur.

Thus we have sought to portray the dynamics of the internal corporate venturing (ICV) process. These are the activities and managerial processes by which R&D developments are moved through and evolve into commercially viable products (or stumble and fail to achieve that viability). While these activities can have a profound impact on the strategy of the corporation, most of what we observed are not top management decisions but "bottom-up" processes. Ideas, proposals, and start-ups typically are initiated at lower levels in the organization and only gradually "percolate" up to the attention of senior management.

In this chapter we want to summarize the major outlines of this process by which radical new innovations get managed in a large corporation. We felt it was important to distinguish the *definition* from the *impetus* process involved in the development of a new venture.[1] In the former, a number of decisions gradually emerge that articulate the technical and economic dimensions of the fledgling new product. Not just sequentially, but often simultaneously it is also necessary to mount an *impetus* process. For this to occur, managers at various levels have to first gain and then maintain support in the corporation for the nascent business.

Continuous impetus allows the activation of the process of *strategic context determination*.[2] Through this process, the corporate strategy is extended to accommodate the new-business activities, which typically fall outside of its current scope. Strategic context determination serves to overcome the hindrances resulting from the firm's *structural context*: the various organizational and administrative mechanisms put in place by corporate management to implement the current corporate strategy.

The Definition of a New Business Opportunity

In storybooks, new ideas appear in a blinding, instantaneous flash of brilliant insight. In reality, the kinds of new-product ideas we explored result from a number of technological breakthroughs that can be occurring inside a corporate R&D laboratory as well as in the wider scientific community. The core of what is innovative typically is produced by an individual or small group that is adept at synthesizing or integrating ideas. Individually these ideas represent new knowledge but not a new product. Combined, they suggest the possibility of a commercial development. That combination gives rise to the distinctive, creative, innovative early "definition" stage.

Linking Processes

We concluded that the greatest potential for commercial development occurs when the definition process begins with a technically trained but entrepreneurially oriented manager tying together or *linking up* several elements of technical knowledge (from inside or outside the lab) that would provide a product or process solution to some preexisting or just-conceived technical problem. For example, by integrating several pieces of ongoing research a scientist might conceive of a new way to separate materials that heretofore had been difficult to purify. This "technical linking" or integration function then needs to be combined with "need linking." Here some new technical solution is shown to be highly useful in serving a market need—either an existing one or one that can be induced. Thus, continuing our previous example, if two materials usually found bound together can be economically separated, that could be the foundation of a new business opportunity for certain kinds of ore processing.

Successful innovations require this *double* linking-up: the tying together of formerly discrete pieces of new technical knowledge and the matching of this newly conceived technical capability with the satisfaction of a market need.

The key individual in this linking process, in our study, turns out to be the first-line supervisor in the corporate R&D department. The effective group leader who can initiate the product development cycle has broad contacts and links, often not only within the laboratory but in the external scientific community. Such people are also, remarkably enough, somewhat conversant with and interested in the business side of the corporation and can begin to conceive of market needs that might be satisified by the emergent technology. Unlike the stereotypes of the scientist who feels cheapened or demeaned by commercial considerations, a critical number of group leader/scientists are enthusiastic about finding potential new products.

138

Product Championing

In addition to linking emergent technological breakthroughs and knowledge and market needs, another function has to be performed at this early stage. The innovative idea has to be nourished by corporate resources or it will wither from lack of support. Because the group leaders are the ones who are most deeply involved in the definition process, they are in the best position to secure corporate resources and support—assuming they have these motivations and personality skills. Thus product championing activities are critical to beginning the impetus process.

The Impetus Process

Persuasive skills, improvising instincts, and risk taking are all required to give an innovation impetus because there is a kind of "catch 22" involved. Frequently innovations don't fit neatly into established categories of expected new products as defined by existing corporate strategy. Many involve products and techniques that customers can't evaluate because they are unlike what they have utilized before. Funding will be very limited because the product has yet to prove itself—but it is also difficult to show results without adequate resources.

Effective product champions create market interest in the new product or process by getting samples or prototypes into customers' hands. At times they cut corners in corporate procedures (e.g., by unauthorized selling from an R&D facility). They may scavenge supplies and materials and equipment from other projects. They may hide or disguise the project because it is not consistent with existing corporate "domains"—until they can show positive results that will encourage upper management to stretch their definitions of corporate interests. Their goal is clear: to get venture status for their embryonic business, to demonstrate that what conventional technical or business wisdom categorized as impossible is actually feasible.

Thus some threshold level of commercial activity is necessary to create a consensus that the innovative activity, heretofore an R&D project, deserves to be upgraded to venture status and shifted to the jurisdiction of the new-business development department. Here it will acquire its own organization, general manager, and operating budget.

While there are formal screening models and their accompanying quantitative techniques, in reality senior management's decision to promote a project to venture status is a highly subjective one. No two projects can be easily judged by identical criteria or by past experience. Much depends on the selling abilities of the product champion—both inside the corporate hierarchy and outside in the marketplace.

Strategic Forcing

In our case studies, the technically oriented product champion then got shifted into the still more demanding position of new-venture manager. It may appear inappropriate that a technically trained manager whose sole experience up to this point was in an R&D environment would be selected for a general management function. However, product champions can be highly motivated to make the transition; many of them, contrary to the popular image of the scientist, are eager to become general managers. Also, there may be no alternative. Management cannot easily find someone with the requisite knowledge about the new product and its potential markets. What is absolutely critical to the new venture is that it not lose momentum by having unnecessary start-up problems such as the training of a new general manager. Furthermore, it must quickly prove itself or top management will grow discouraged and it will not qualify for the support necessary to launch the new venture properly.

What then occurs in successful ventures we have called "strategic forcing." Strategic forcing is an effort of gaining market penetration and showing consistent, impressive growth at almost any cost. Thus in one of our cases, the new venture doubled its sales volume every year for 5 consecutive years. The new-venture management established an international operation at the same time as they were starting up domestically and did a number of things simultaneously that might normally have been started only sequentially. Venture managers learn that to retain top management's support and to encourage others in the corporation to be cooperative who might have to provide services, parts, or materials, they have to look like winners.

The old saws about the rich getting richer and success breeding success seem to apply. If the venture looks like a winner, people will do things to support it that will help make it a success. In contrast, if there are early technical or marketing problems that slow the growth rate, support will be less forthcoming, which will make it harder to overcome those handicaps. We may be dealing here with a self-fulfilling prophecy: the suspicion that you might be a failure helps guarantee that you will be. Often the fate of the venture is sealed when management sends in new, inexperienced venture managers or "helpers," indicating a lack of confidence in the former product champion. His or her diminished status and influence is often the beginning of the end.

Strategic Neglect

The "flip side" of successful strategic forcing is "strategic neglect" of the development of the administrative infrastructure for the new venture. Only those aspects of the business that are seen as relevant to fast growth get any serious attention. Thus even new-product development (ironically enough) and the development of new complementary products and services get neglected, as does the introduction of management specialists in such fields as manufacturing, purchasing, and so forth. Instead the venture gets along "on the cheap" by utilizing a small number of generalists who cover many bases. Eventually this short-sighted approach builds up costs that can't be ignored. For example, the original product that spawned the new venture begins to age, or it becomes obvious that there should be a broader line of products and services. At some point new specialists may be added to round out the administrative framework, but they are likely to meet resistance from the entrepreneurially inclined venture manager who is being pressured to show rapid growth and has no time to improve the infrastructure. Conflicts between functional needs and the general manager's push toward fast growth will be destructive. While development of functions like manufacturing will pay off in the long run, the venture manager is interested only in short-run market penetration.

At some point, the venture manager, who in response to external and internal pressures becomes so narrowly focused and is driven to increase sales volume at any cost, will either have to change or be replaced. Frequently at this stage such individuals are unable to shift mental gears; the opposite behavior has been reinforced for too long. These "growth-at-any-cost" managers are then replaced with less-entrepreneurial-type managers, who are interested in longer-run technical and administrative development. It is indeed tragic that the entrepreneurial venture manager can easily become a casualty in the process of fulfilling his or her appointed mission: gaining a beach-head in an unfriendly marketplace. The more successful the entrepreneurial venture manager in gaining the sales volume, the greater is the likelihood that he or she will be unsuccessful at doing the administrative development efforts that will have great value in the longer run.

Strategic Building

In new ventures that evolved into viable commercial successes, one could see the contribution of "strategic building." Usually performed by a higher level of management (the manager of the venture manager), this involves articulating and implementing a master strategy for the business. Going way beyond improving sales volumes of the core product, the strategy seeks to construct a multi-product business and a view of relevant markets that would carry the venture forward to the point where it could become a free-standing operating unit. This would include carefully articulated written strategic plans submitted to top management that identify current problems and long-run opportunities.

Central to these plans is the agglomeration and/or the acquisition of related products and technologies to complement and fill out a line of products and services. Some may come from other parts of the corporation; others will represent acquisitions. Both require persuading senior management of the wisdom of the transfer or the appropriation of funds.

In most corporations the ability of the venture to gain this kind of support will depend upon gaining the confidence of top management. That, in turn, will be a function of the predictability of the venture. Has the venture's management been able to portray accurately in their planning the problems faced and then been able to solve them in succeeding accounting periods? And, second, have the acquisitions had predicted results? When the answers to both questions are in the affirmative, continuing financial support for the cash-absorbing new venture will be forthcoming. Unpredictable but hungry new ventures soon get starved.

While strategic building often gets initiated by a level of management above the new venture, there are really two styles of management apparent at this stage. Given the willingness of the middle-level manager (and provided he or she has the time available) to act as coach and the responsiveness and ability of the venture manager to learn broader managerial skills, the impetus process will represent a combined effort. Regrettably, in most of the cases we observed persistent-coaching did not take place, and the venture manager eventually was overwhelmed by the strategic forcing (and concomitant strategic neglect) and had to be replaced. It is difficult to say who was at fault. Was there inadequate effort devoted to coaching or stubborn unwillingness to learn or both? Or was there just not time to do both well?

Organizational Championing

Whoever performs the strategic building activities also engages in what we have called "organizational championing." Given the competing demands on top management's time, the inherent ambiguities involved in evaluating the performance of a new venture without much of a track record, and the inevitable unanticipated crises and blunders, someone has to persuade top management that *this* venture is worthwhile. This requires establishing and maintaining reasonably regular contact with top management, keeping them well informed, and developing their enthusiasm for this particular new activity.

This kind of championing is largely a political activity. The head of new-business development often has to commit his or her judgment (in terms that can be verified as being right or wrong) and put his or her reputation on the line in saying that a particular venture will be successful if it is properly supported. Cautious but astute organizational champions make sure that the causes (i.e., new ventures) they sponsor are consistent with the existing predispositions of top management. More brilliant or perhaps more risk-prone executives seek to change the disposition of top management and get them to accept a *new* business field as legitimate for corporate development. Part of their success is probably simply a function of personality and persistence, of being able to be enthusiastic and appearing confident and articulate in explaining and justifying one's position. But there is also an intellectual component, as we have seen: successful organizational champions are able to devise a suitable overall long-run strategy for a business and perceive new ventures in strategic terms, in contrast to the technical terms used by product champions.

Strategic Context

In effect, these middle-level managers in new-venture development by their organizational championing activities are reshaping the corporate strategy. Their initiatives, when successful, change the direction(s) and the strategic plans of the corporation. Organizational championing means getting top management to modify existing corporate strategy in order to accommodate a successful new venture. Thus, relatively autonomous, unplanned initiatives from the operational and middle levels of the organization help to shape corporate strategy.

Delineating

Top management picks and chooses among these initiatives and thereby legitimates them, but the basic thrust comes from below, not from above. This modification of strategy is necessary for several reasons:

1. The new venture can represent an area of activity (domain) not considered legitimate by the existing strategy.
2. Often the new venture entails activities and/or generates values—or a culture—that is inconsistent with the existing direction and ideas of the present corporation.
3. Top management may well be aware that its current strategy is not entirely adequate but doesn't know how to change it.

Thus new fields of business activity for the corporation to pursue are delineated as a result of middle-level managers' efforts to integrate into a new strategic framework the initiatives put forth by operational-level managers who are seeking to grow new ventures inside the corporation.

Retroactive Rationalizing

Apparently and understandably, nonconformity with existing strategies and values cannot be tolerated indefinitely in the large business organization which seeks predictable systems and bounded strategies. To cope with the kind of divergencies we have been describing, top management needs to retroactively give legitimacy to what has been going on in these new ventures by making appropriate changes in the corporate strategy. This makes legitimate the new line of business that would otherwise be nonconforming. But the significant element in terms of the dynamics of these diversified firms is that strategy changes come *after* the successful experiment, not *before*.

Many autonomous strategic initiatives compete for survival. (The young ventures learn that they can best compete by fast growth and visible size.) Strategic choice in these corporations takes place through experimentation and selection rather than through top management's strategic planning. This provides a far different and perhaps a far more optimistic and viable view of innovation in the large organization than the traditional model. It would be difficult to imagine much real innovation occurring in large businesses that had to rely on those changes being foreseen and preordained by prescient plans made by top management.

Structural Context

Given the limited involvement of corporate management in the process of strategic context determination, how do they try to exert control over the ICV process? Our study suggests that they do so by structuring the internal selection environment.

Structuring

Corporate management relies on the determination of the structural context in its attempts to influence the strategic process concerning ICV. The structural context includes the diverse organizational and administrative elements whose manipulation is likely to affect the perception of the strategic actors concerning what needs to be done to gain corporate support for particular initiatives. The creation of the NVD as a separate organizational unit, the definition of positions and responsibilities in the departments of the NVD, the establishment of criteria for measuring and evaluating the performance of both the venture and the venture manager, and the assignment of either entrepreneurially or administratively inclined managers to key positions in the NVD all are intended to affect the course of ICV activity.

The corporate level is the dominant force in the determination of structural context. Corporate management's manipulations of the structural context are guided primarily by strategic concerns at their level, reflecting emphasis on either expansion of mainstream business or diversification, depending on perceptions at different times of the prospects of current mainstream businesses.

These changes in structural context do not often reflect a well-conceived strategy for diversification, and seem primarily aimed at consolidating ICV efforts at different levels of activity rather than at guiding and directing these efforts. In the company we studied, the NVD was created in the early 1970s because people in the divisions had been engaging in what some managers called a "wild spree" of diversification efforts. Corporate management wanted to consolidate these efforts, although at a relatively high level of activity. Key managers involved in those earlier decisions pointed out that the direction of these consolidated efforts was based on preceding lower-level initiatives that had created resource commitments, rather than on a clear corporate strategy of diversification.

The lack of clear strategy for directing diversification was also evident in our study in 1977, when significant changes in the functioning of the NVD took place. The newly appointed NVD manager pointed out that corporate management had not expressed clear guiding principles for further diversification beyond the emphasis on consolidation and the need to reduce the number of fields in which ICV activity was taking place.

Selecting

Structural context determination thus remains a rather crude tool for influencing ICV efforts. It results in an internal selection environment in which the autonomous strategic initiatives emerging from below compete for survival. In all the ICV cases in our study, strong signals of fast growth and large size as criteria for survival were read into the structural context by the participants. This affected the process, if not so much the specific content, of their behavior. The importance of product championing, strategic forcing, strategic building, and the corresponding forms of strategic neglect seems to indicate this. The inherent crudeness of the structural context as a tool for influencing the ICV process provided, of course, the rationale as well as the opportunity for the activation of the strategic context determination process discussed earlier.

Key and Peripheral Activities in the Venturing Process

Our description of the ICV process in this chapter has been different from the description in terms of "stages" provided in the preceding chapters.[3] In this chapter, we have pulled together the strategic activities of different levels of management involved in the venturing process. We have focused our discussion on what appear to be the key activities that take place at the different levels of management simultaneously as well as sequentially. We have shown how these activities interlock with each other, and have discussed some major problems related to the various forms of strategic neglect which arise in the network of strategic activities. The emphasis on key activities should not, however, lead us to ignore the more *peripheral* activities that we have observed. We believe strongly that those peripheral activities need to gain in relative importance in order to manage the ICV process better. (See Chapter 10.)

To provide a complete picture of the activities constituting the ICV process, we have constructed a "process model" which is presented in Figure 9-1.

Corporate management monitored the resource allocation to emerging ICV projects. Middle-level managers managed these resources and facilitated collaboration between R&D and business people in the definition of new business opportunities; however, these activities seemed to support rather than drive the definition process. In the same fashion, *authorizing* further development was clearly the prerogative of corporate management, but this was a result not a determinant of the impetus process. In the strategic context determination process, *gatekeeping*, *idea generating*, and *bootlegging* activities by operational-level participants were all found to be important in developing a basis for further definition processes. In the process of

Figure 9-1

Key and Peripheral Activities in a Process Model of ICV (*Reprinted from "A Process Model of Internal Corporate Venturing in the Diversified Major Firm" by R. A. Burgelman published in Administrative Science Quarterly, June 1983, by permission of The Administrative Science Quarterly. Copyright 1983 Cornell University.*)

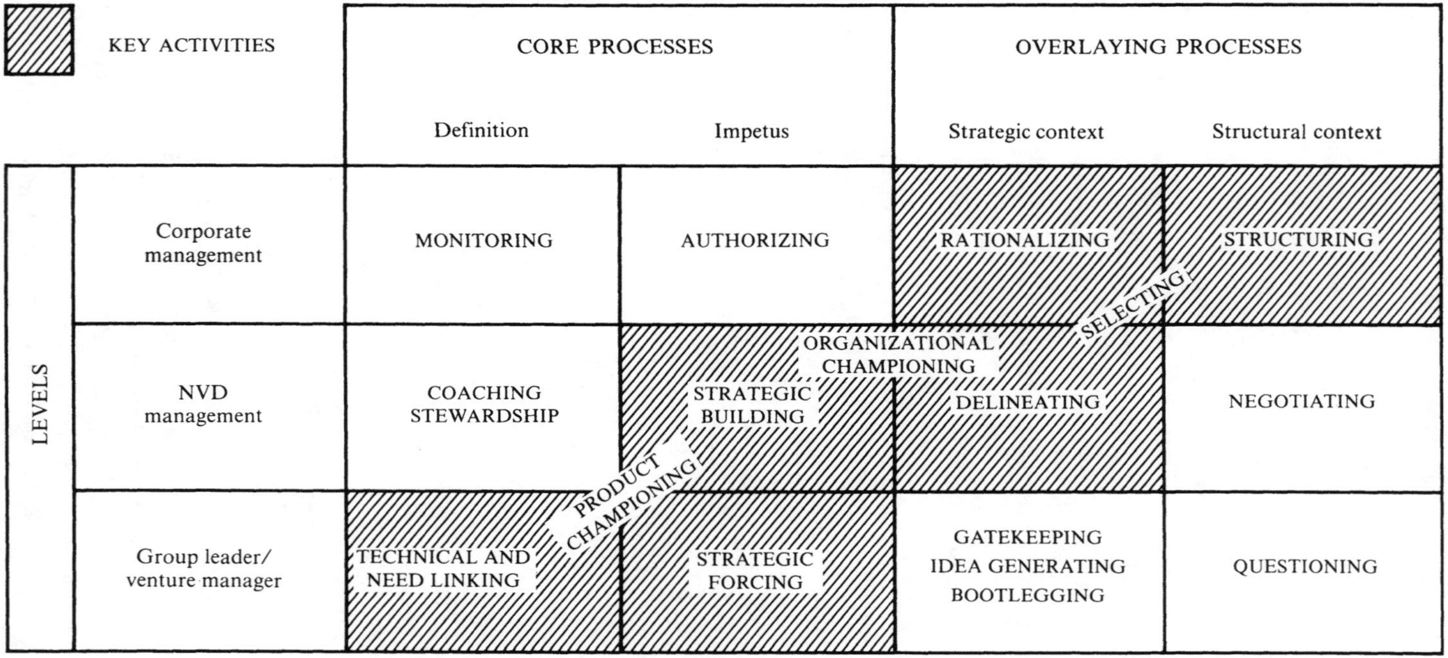

KEY ACTIVITIES	CORE PROCESSES		OVERLAYING PROCESSES	
	Definition	Impetus	Strategic context	Structural context
Corporate management	MONITORING	AUTHORIZING	RATIONALIZING	STRUCTURING
NVD management	COACHING STEWARDSHIP	STRATEGIC BUILDING	ORGANIZATIONAL CHAMPIONING / DELINEATING	NEGOTIATING
Group leader/ venture manager	TECHNICAL AND NEED LINKING	STRATEGIC FORCING	GATEKEEPING IDEA GENERATING BOOTLEGGING	QUESTIONING

Diagonal labels: PRODUCT CHAMPIONING; SELECTING

LEVELS

148

structural context determination, *questioning* of the structural context by operational-level participants and efforts by middle managers to *negotiate* changes in it seemed to be reactive rather than primary.

Four Key Problem Areas in the ICV Process

The process model presented in this chapter provides a framework for identifying *four* major problems areas in the strategic management of ICV. These include, first, *vicious circles* in the definition process: resources could be obtained if technical feasibility was demonstrated for a project but such demonstration itself required resources. Similar problems arose in relation to efforts to demonstrate commercial feasibility. Even when a technically demonstrated product, process, or system existed, corporate management was often reluctant to start commercialization efforts because they were unsure about the firm's capabilities to effectively do so. These vicious circles require an extreme emphasis on product championing on the part of project initiators. The process model allows us to show the lack of articulation between the activities of different levels of management, which may account to a large extent for the vicious circles encountered in the definition process.

A second problem area concerns *managerial dilemmas* within the impetus process. The venture manager's dilemma is maximizing growth with the product, process, or system available versus developing the functional capabilities of the embryonic business organization. For the middle-level manager the dilemma is focusing on expanding the scope of the new business versus spending time coaching the (often recalcitrant) venture manager. The process model allows us to show how the strategic situation at each level of management in the impetus process is different, with fast growth being the main shared interest.

Third, there is a high level of *indeterminateness in the strategic context* of ICV. Strategic guidance on the part of top management is limited to declaring corporate interest in broadly defined fields like "health" or "energy." Also, there is a tendency for severe oscillation in top management's interest in ICV: a "now we like it, now we don't" type of approach. It looks very much as if new ventures are viewed by top management as insurance against mainstream business going bad rather than as a corporate objective per se. In the determination or strategic context, even more than in the impetus process, the strategies of the various levels of management show a lack of articulation with each other. The process model again allows us to depict this.

Fourth, the structural context tends to exert *perverse selective pressures* on the venture to grow fast which exacerbate the external environmental pressures. Changes in top management orientation toward expansion or consolidation of ICV activity seem to lead to reactive changes in the structuring of the NVD. Because of the widely shared perception that the position of the NVD is precarious, an attitude of "it's now or never" is created on the part of the participants, adding to the pressures on the venture to grow fast. This also can be depicted in the process model.

To be sure, these four problem areas are not exhaustive or independent of each other. However, they do draw attention to issues that are often overlooked because of the embeddedness of managerial activities and the difficulty of conceptualizing the dynamics of managerial activities simultaneously at multiple levels of analysis. The process model provides a tool for revealing this embeddedness and representing in a reasonably simple, yet encompassing, way the intricate dynamics of *organizational* strategy making.

Conclusion

The process model can be used as a flexible tool for examining and elucidating ICV activities in large, established firms. It can help companies involved in ICV to map out their strategic management approach. Companies thus can examine the extent to which the key problems exist in their organization. Different companies may find that they experience only certain of these problems and some other problems as well. This may be because they are managing ICV somewhat differently or because the nature of their ICV activities is somewhat different.

We believe that a process model conceptualization thus can help top management understand *better and more completely* the deeply rooted problems and, indeed, the "perverse dynamics" generated and encountered by internal corporate venturing.

In Chapter 10 we will propose some recommendations to alleviate, if not eliminate, these major problems and perverse dynamics in managing the ICV process.

CHAPTER 10

Management Strategies
That Improve the Odds

A serious effort to create innovative new ventures inside a corporation with many routinized activities and businesses is a major challenge. Meeting it successfully not only provides a method of restocking an aging or obsolete business portfolio, but it also teaches management many lessons of more general value about how to run a large organization. Such organizations are prone to the ills of bureaucracies: rigid procedures, hierarchy-bound slowness of response, and difficulty in coping with change whether external or internal. They often purposely or inadvertently discourage entrepreneurially minded executives with a will to achieve and build.

In looking at the problems of establishing and maintaining the vitality of an autonomous new-ventures activity dedicated to incubating radical new innovations, we can see in microcosm many of the problems of encouraging innovation in the large diversified organization.

Having identified major problems associated with the use of the NVD (see Chapter 8), and with the strategic process regarding ICV (see Chapter 9), recommendations for improving the strategic management of ICV can be proposed. They serve to alleviate if not eliminate the problems, by making the corporate context more hospitable to ICV. Corresponding to the four major problem areas in managing the ICV process are four "themes" for our recommendations:

1. Facilitating the definition process
2. Moderating the impetus process
3. Elaborating the strategic context of ICV
4. Refining the structural context of ICV

These recommendations are summarized in Table 10–1.

Facilitating the Definition Process

Timely assessment of the true potential of an ICV project remains a difficult problem. This follows from the very nature of such projects: the many uncertainties concerning the technical and marketing aspects of the new business and the fact that each case is significantly different from all others. These factors make it quite difficult to develop standardized evaluation procedures and development programs without screening to death truly innovative projects.

Managing the definition process effectively poses serious challenges for middle-level managers in the corporate R&D department. They must facilitate the integration of technical and business perspectives and must maintain a lifeline to the technology developed in corporate R&D as the project takes off. As stated earlier, the need for product championing efforts, if excessive, may cut that lifeline early on and lead to severe discontinuities in new-product development after the project has reached the venture stage. The middle-level manager's efforts must facilitate both the product championing efforts and the continued development of the technology base by putting the former in perspective and making sure that the interface between R&D and business people works smoothly.

Facilitating the Integration of the R&D and Business Perspectives

To facilitate the integration of technical and business perspectives, the middle manager must understand the operating logic of both groups. He must avoid getting bogged down in technical details yet

Table 10-1
Recommendations for Making ICV Strategy Work Better

| Levels | Core Processes | | Overlaying Processes | |
	Definition	Impetus	Strategic Context	Structural Context
Corporate management	ICV proposals are evaluated in light of corporate development strategy. Conscious efforts are made to avoid subjecting them to conventional corporate wisdom.	New-venture progress is evaluated in substantive terms by top managers who have experience in organizational championing.	A process is in place for developing long-term corporate development strategy. This strategy takes shape as result of ongoing interactive learning process involving top and middle levels of management.	Managers with successful ICV experience are appointed to top management. Top management is rewarded financially and symbolically for long-term corporate development success.
NVD management	Middle-level managers in corporate R&D are selected who have both technical depth and business knowledge necessary to determine minimum amount of resources for project, and who can coach star players.	Middle-level managers are responsible for use and development of venture managers as scarce resources of corporation, and they facilitate intrafirm project transfers if new-business strategy warrants it.	Substantive interaction between corporate and middle-level management leads to clarifying merits of new business field in light of corporate development strategy.	Star performers at middle level are attracted to ICV activities. Collaboration of mainstream middle level with ICV activities is rewarded. Integrating mechanisms can easily be mobilized.

153

Table 10-1 (Cont.)

Levels	Core Processes		Overlaying Processes	
	Definition	Impetus	Strategic Context	Structural Context
Group leader/ venture leader	Project initiators are encouraged to integrate technical and business perspectives. They are provided access to resources. Project initiators can be rewarded by means other than promotion to venture manager.	Venture managers are responsible for developing functional capabilities of emerging venture organizations and for codification of what has been learned in terms of required functional capabilities while pursuing new business opportunity.	Slack resources determine level of emergence of mutant ideas. Existence of substantive corporate development strategy provides preliminary self-selection of mutant ideas.	A wide array of venture structures and supporting measurement and reward systems clarifies expected performance for ICV personnel.

Source: Reprinted from "Managing the Internal Corporate Venturing Process," by R. A. Burgelman, *Sloan Management Review*, Vol. 25, No. 2, Figure 10, by permission of the publisher. Copyright © 1984 by the Sloan Management Review Association. All rights reserved.

must have sufficient technical depth to command the respect of the R&D people. Such managers must be able to motivate the R&D people to collaborate with the business people toward the formulation of business objectives against which progress can be measured. Formulating adequate business objectives is especially important if corporate management becomes more actively involved in ICV and develops a greater capacity to evaluate how new projects fit in with the corporate development strategy.

Middle-level managers in R&D must be capable of facilitating give-and-take between the two groups in a process of mutual adjustment toward the common goal of advancing the progress of the new-business project. Of key importance in this regard is creating mutual respect between technical and business people. If the R&D manager sets the example by showing respect for the business people's contribution this is likely to have a carry-over effect on the attitudes of the other R&D people. Regular meetings between the two groups to evaluate, as peers, the contribution of the different members of the team is likely to lead to more integrated efforts.

The Middle Manager as Coach

Such meetings also provide a vehicle for better coaching the product champion. The latter is really the driving force behind the ICV project at this stage of development. There are some similarities between this role and that of the star player on a sports team. Often the situation with respect to product champions as star players is viewed in either/or terms. Either he or she can "do their thing," and then chances are that we will succeed, but there will be discontinuities and not fully exploited ancillary opportunities; or we can "harness" the product champion but then he or she won't play.

A more balanced approach is possible if the middle-level manager uses a process in which the product champion is recognized as the star player, but is, at times, challenged to maintain breadth by having to respond to queries like:

- How is the team benefiting more from this particular action than from others that the team may think are important?
- How will the continuity of the efforts of the team be preserved?
- What will be the next step?

155

To back up this approach, the middle manager should have a say in how to reward the participants in an ICV project differently. This, of course, refers back to the determination of the structural context (see below), and reemphasizes the importance at the corporate level of recognizing that different reward systems are necessary for different types of activities involved in ICV.

Coping with Unanticipated Technical Problems

Any new product or service will be plagued with a wide and unanticipated variety of startup problems. It is easy to forget how many such "bugs" have been eliminated over the years in existing products. For example, the ideal material begins to deteriorate with heat; two parts, given the slightest variation in dimension, interfere with each other; a particular fabrication process that worked perfectly with a similar product will not consistently produce acceptable quality; and so on.

What is of importance to management is not the ability to predict these technical problems; most can't be predicted, no matter how well-planned is the changeover process, or how careful is the ongoing testing. Rather, what is critical is the response. In the definition process, two typical responses are fatal to the long-run success of a new venture.

The first is to presume that someone is to blame and then proceed to seek out the "culprit." The temptation to do this is strong when an unforeseen problem is delaying delivery of one of the first orders, raising costs way above estimates, and threatening the very reputation of the fledgling venture's performance. If either the venture management or corporate management, having grown fearful that optimistic projected targets of sales or costs aren't being met, panics and seeks to place blame and punish those who have made a mistake, a number of deleterious consequences follow from this course of "management by autopsy" (as some call it):

1. Fearing retribution and seeking to avoid prosecution, each individual or unit seeks to prove its work or plan is not the source of the problem. "If everyone else had done as they should have, the problem would not have occurred" is the party line. Furthermore, everyone knows that agreeing to change one of their specifications or procedures is tantamount to admitting guilt, admitting they were wrong.

Thus, at the very time when there should be some looseness in the organization and individuals and groups should be seeking to assist one another in making the whole product work, each is holding firm to its own plans.

> Ideally, this is what should occur: A new extruder is not producing the finish that was anticipated. However, if the next process in line can add one additional step in its work procedure, that level of finishing can be achieved. However, that extra step will increase their labor costs, require a change in their budgeted allowances, and at the outset it will slow their output. This creates some problems for the sales staff seeking rapid installation in the first customer's premises. A whole series of trade-offs involving compromises and adjustments among several units and consultations with the customer should take place with the final plan reflecting the larger interests of the project and not the special and "local" interests of any of the participants.

This type of rolling adjustment and change in plans and specifications is a constant in new-product development, but it won't take place when the participants fear that concessions will be held against them or are an admission of guilt in the origination of the problem that set off the issue. Such concessions are also discouraged when management presumes that no such issues would arise if there had been more careful planning in the first place and someone "goofed" in the original designs who ought to be penalized.

2. Alternatively, in their haste to get early sales and installations, new-product managers seek to ignore, hide, or gloss over early difficulties. Often the rationalization is that every new product is defective and the difficulties can be solved by "retrofitting" later either on the customer's premises or at the end of the line. Such tactics discourage early customers, demoralize staff, and accustom the entire new venture to less-than-perfect quality and poor standards. The start-up period is crucial for identifying flaws in materials, methods, or the design itself, and if not solved at that stage these problems will haunt and potentially destroy the credibility of the new venture at a later stage.

> Ideally, this is what should occur: One of the authors witnessed how NASA handled the development of a new satellite. After a failure occurred, every manufacturing stage and component was examined. Through meticulous record keeping and analysis the Agency was able to determine that the component which had failed had been assembled in a

specific location during the afternoon of a particular day on which a truck had happened to be parked near a duct leading to a "clean room." The exhaust from the truck's engine had produced particles which interfered with the performance of a finely tuned electronic part. The air circulation system was improved and no vehicles were allowed near the building as a result of the investigation.[1]

Thus successful new-venture management involves being sensitive to and being able to track down every unanticipated problem but utilizing a style that avoids seeking to punish "culprits" or rushing through faulty production. The purpose of the definition process is ultimately to maximize the probability of success of the project in a situation of great uncertainty about technical, marketing, and organizational conditions.

Moderating the Impetus Process

Once a project obtains venture status, corporate management should expect the middle-level managers involved to think and act as corporate strategists and the operational-level managers to view themselves as organization builders.

Middle-Level Managers as Corporate Strategists

Strategy making in new ventures depends to a very great extent on the middle-level managers. Because new ventures often intersect with multiple parts of the mainstream businesses, middle managers learn what the corporate capabilities and skills are—and the shortcomings in them—and learn to articulate new strategies and build new businesses based on new combinations of corporate capabilities and skills. This, in turn, also creates possibilities for enhancing the realization of new operational synergies existing in the firm. Middle-level managers can thus serve as agents toward facilitating crucial integrations and technology transfers within the corporation, and corporate management should expect them to perform this role as they develop the new-venture strategy.

An excellent example of the middle-level manager as corporate strategist is provided by Renn Zaphiropoulos, who explained how he integrated his organization (Versatec) in the corporate structure after it had been acquired by Xerox[2]:

> "When we first became members of Xerox, nobody knew why they bought us," he recalls. In such a case, he thinks, "you don't wait for the corporate guys to do it. You know that to make it right depends on you primarily." His strategy was to visit all of Xerox's research facilities regularly to find out what they were doing that Versatec could use.

For internal ventures such "reaching out" and "weaving things together" would seem to be equally important.

There is another related organizational lesson here. As with most successful managerial practices, there needs to be a balance between what appear to be contradictory approaches. There is the need to shelter and protect the fledgling new venture. Also, a small group of dedicated "true believers" can work miracles through the commitments generated by group dynamics and identification with "their" product in "their" miniature company. But this isolation can go too far, and there also needs to be exposure to outsiders. There is a vast range of experience, technology, and resources available in the larger organization that must be shared. Furthermore, outsiders can introduce important new ideas and raise critical questions in areas that appear too simple or too "cut and dried" to a somewhat incestuous small group of insiders. At one and the same time, the new venture needs the protection that an infant industry must have, while it also requires some openness to the world of ideas existing outside itself. The role of the middle-level manager is to consider all of these aspects, and to make the necessary trade-offs bearing in mind the corporate strategic interest in the venture throughout what we have termed the impetus process.

The Venture Manager as Organization Builder

Pursuing fast growth as well as administrative development of the venture simultaneously is a major challenge during the impetus process. This challenge, which exists for any start-up business, is especially treacherous for one in the context of an established firm. This is so because managers in ICV typically have less control over the selection of key venture personnel yet, at the same time, have more ready access to a wide array of corporate resources. Thus, there seems to be less pressure on the venture managers and the middle-level manager to show progress in building the organization than there is to show growth.

The recommendations (see below) concerning measurement and rewards systems should encourage the venture manager to balance the two concerns better. The venture manager should have leeway in hiring and firing decisions, but should also be held responsible for the development of new functional capabilities and the administrative framework of the venture. This would reduce the probability of major discountinuities in new-product development documented in preceding chapters. In addition, it would provide the corporation with codified know-how and information which can be transferred to other parts of the firm, or to other new ventures, even if one from which it is derived ultimately fails as a business. Know-how and information contributing to "organizational learning" thus become important outputs of the ICV process, in addition to sales and profit dollars.[3]

Often, the product champion/venture manager will not have the required capabilities to achieve these additional objectives. The availability of compensatory rewards and of avenues for recycling the product champion/venture manager would make it possible for middle management to tackle deteriorating managerial conditions in the new-business organization with greater fortitude. Furthermore, the availability of a competent replacement (as a result of systematic corporate search) may induce the product champion/venture manager to relinquish his or her position rather than see the venture go under.

Elaborating the Strategic Context of ICV

Determining the strategic context of ICV is a subtle and somewhat elusive process involving corporate and middle-level managers. More effort should be spent on developing a long-term corporate development strategy explicitly encompassing ICV. This should be paralleled by measures to increase corporate management's capacity to assess venture strategies in substantive terms as well as in terms of projected quantitative results. Top management should develop the capacity to apply an experimentation-and-selection approach to the strategic management of ICV.

160

The Need for a Corporate Development Strategy

Top management should recognize that ICV is an important source of strategic renewal for the firm, and does not work well if used as "insurance" against poor mainstream business prospects. ICV should therefore be considered an integral and continuous part of the strategy-making process. To dampen the oscillations in corporate support for ICV, top management should create a process for developing an explicit long-term (10 to 12 years) strategy for corporate development, supported by a strategy for resource generation and allocation. Both should be based on ongoing efforts to determine the remaining growth opportunities in the current mainstream businesses and the resource levels necessary to exploit them. Given the corporate objectives for growth and profitability, a resource pool should be reserved for activities outside the mainstream business. This pool should not be affected by short-term fluctuations in current mainstream activities. The existence of this pool of "slack" (or perhaps better, "uncommitted") resources would allow top management to affect the rate at which new-venture initiatives will emerge, if not their particular content. This approach reflects a broader concept of strategy making than allotting a certain percentage of revenues derived from sales as the budget for maintaining corporate R&D.

Substantive Assessment of Venture Strategies

To more effectively determine the strategic context of ICV, and to reduce the political emphasis in organizational championing activities, top management should increase its capacity to make substantive assessments of the merits of new ventures for corporate development. Top management should learn to better assess the *strategic importance* to corporate development and the *degree of relatedness* to core corporate capabilities of ICV projects (see chapter 11 for an elaboration of these two dimensions). One way to achieve this capacity is for top management to include members with significant experience in new-business development in the top management team.[4] In addition, top management should require middle-level organizational champions to explain how a new field of business would further the corporate development objectives in substantive rather than purely numerical terms; in other words, how they expect the new-business

161

fields they champion to create value from the corporate point of view. Operational-level managers would then be able to assess better which of the possible directions their envisaged projects could take will be more likely to receive corporate support.

Managing Through Experimentation and Selection

An important lesson for management is the role of what we have called autonomous strategic initiatives. With the enormous emphasis on planning that has developed over the past two decades, it has been easy to presume that future directions could be shaped solely be senior management's analysis and prescience. In turn, such plans appear to provide a reassuring framework according to which the firm can pursue growth in an orderly and rational fashion.

However, given the assured uncertainty of the future—of unpredicted and unpredictable changes in technology, governmental regulations, competitors' behavior, and users' preferences—a viable organization requires experimental diversity as well as plans. One of the best ways of facilitating the emergence of the diversity that will produce innovative products and technologies is to take advantage of the entrepreneurial initiatives that are likely to arise spontaneously (and autonomously) at the operational levels. That in turn means allowing middle-level managers who are close to markets and emerging technologies to fuse their knowledge of technological possibilities and user interests into new-product possibilities. Corporate strategy then becomes in part the end result of an experimentation and selection process. This contrasts sharply with the more orderly, planned-out way of identifying winners and losers in advance.[5]

It is undoubtedly difficult for senior managers to step back and accept the role of being able to *recognize* viable unanticipated strategic initiatives in contrast to *planning* them. However, by allowing middle-level managers to redefine the strategic context and by becoming fast learners, top management can make sure that entrepreneurial activities will correspond to their strategic vision retroactively. Thus, top management can control the rate of change and the balance between diversity (experimental innovations) and order (existing, "tried and true" product lines). The specific content of the entrepreneurial activity grows out of the highly motivated efforts of these middle- and operational-level managers who are seeking opportunistically to "ride" a new conception into a major career advance. In brief, top management should be more interested in process—managing the evolution of strategy and anticipating that some share of the actual content of plans will evolve by trial and error without the precision and elegance of traditional strategic planning.

Without this diversity and the unanticipated innovations that grow out of a carefully nurtured entrepreneurial culture embedded within a more routinized culture, large organizations are unlikely to weather the growing turbulence of their environments. Inevitably top management's own strategies will be limited by their shared experiences, often reflecting an earlier historical period and even common roots. Furthermore, given the range of uncertainties surrounding new-product development, particularly when considering radical innovations—products outside the firm's historical experience—selection only makes sense *after* innovations have been allowed a chance to flourish. Those that "take" can get long-run support; those that wither get pruned.

Our observations also cast into doubt the practice of seeking to make significant innovational breakthroughs "to order." While there certainly will be times when concerted efforts lead to predetermined goals, many companies have been frustrated when they sought a specific new product with certain prescribed characteristics that would not be derivative.

Aside from the difficulty of predicting real technological breakthroughs, there can be organizational impediments to inventing a product "to order." Usually such an effort represents a high priority on the part of the company, and upper management gives the early stages undue attention. Thus, approvals are required by the managerial hierarchy at predetermined checkpoints, and it is likely that truly new ideas will be discouraged and/or early impediments will cause panic if too rapid changes in direction are required.

Refining the Structural Context of ICV

Refining the structural context requires corporate management to use the new-venture division design in a more deliberate fashion, and to complement the organization design effort with supporting incentive (reward) systems. The latter imply an increase in top management's capacity to evaluate and appraise managerial performance as it relates to innovative activities.

More Deliberate Use of the New-Venture Division Design

Corporate management should develop greater flexibility in structuring the relationship between new-venture projects and the corporation. In some cases, for instance, greater efforts would seem to be in order to integrate new-venture projects directly into the mainstream businesses, rather than transferring them to the NVD because of lack of support in the operating division where they originated. In other instances, projects should be developed using external venture arrangements. Where and how a new-venture project is developed should depend on top management's assessment of its strategic importance for the firm and of the degree to which the required capabilities are related to the firm's core capabilities. Such assessment should be made easier to implement by making a wide range of structures for venture–corporation interrelationships available.[6] (In Chapter 11 we shall discuss the range of options in more detail.)

Also, the NVD is a mechanism for decoupling the activities of new ventures and those of mainstream businesses. However, this decoupling usually cannot be perfect. Hence, integrative mechanisms (e.g., "steering committees" involving managers from operating divisions and the NVD) should be established to deal constructively with the conflicts that will unavoidably and unpredictably arise.

Finally, top management should facilitate greater acceptance of differences between the management processes of the NVD and mainstream businesses. This may lead, for instance, to more careful personnel assignment policies and to greater flexibility in hiring and firing policies in the NVD to reflect the special needs of emerging businesses.

Incentives for Top Management to Support ICV

Perhaps the most difficult aspect concerns how to provide incentives for top management to seriously and continuously support ICV as part of corporate strategy making. The total development cycle from inception to free-standing new business may take 10 years or more. American management, in part because of pressure from the stock market, or perhaps because of a "congenital factor," is not known for its patience, however. Managers often confuse legitimate impatience with the desire to "rush" things. Given the likelihood of unanticipated technical problems and the need to be responsible to changing market reactions (which will keep changing as the product takes shape, particularly if it is truly innovative), senior management must allow adequate time. New products grow and develop slowly. It is much less expensive to undertake a variety of technical and marketing experiments in the developmental stage than to make major capital investments in capacity based on faulty premises.

Obviously, there will be times when there is a race to get into the market first with a product when competitors are in hot pursuit. Of course, one could add parenthetically that when the product is flawed or its marketing is flawed, being first may not assure preeminence in the market. Companies that are going to be successful at radical product innovation need to find ways of communicating realistic time horizons to their innovation "champions" that allow a distinctive rhythm or tempo of organizational activity. This is not quite the contemplative laboratory model, but it also isn't the constant crisis atmosphere, the round-the-clock frenetic pace that ought to be the unusual rather than the modal pattern.

Writing a corporate history might be an effective way to encourage this.[7] It would involve the careful documentation and periodic publication (e.g., as a special section in the annual report) of decisions the positive or negative results of which became clear only 10 or more years after the fact. Corporate leaders (like political ones) would presumably make efforts to preserve their position in corporate history. Another mechanism is to attract "top performers" in the mainstream businesses of the corporation to ICV activities. To do so, at least a few spots on the top management team should always be filled by managers who have had significant experience in new-business development. As noted earlier, this will facilitate the determination of the strategic context for ICV. It will also eliminate the perception that NVD participants are not part of the real world, and thus have not much chance to advance in the corporation as a result of ICV experience.

Performance Evaluation and Reward Systems

Rewards presuppose the ability to evaluate or appraise. There is probably too much emphasis on the "bottom line" in evaluating managers in new ventures. While every sensible assessment of the new-product development process recognizes that there may be a 10- or 15-year lag between the early stages and real profitability, firms still seem short-term oriented and look for profit surrogates when there aren't real profits. As we noted in our study of United, in the case of "good" new ventures, new-venture managers see sales volume double each year. This places great pressure on them to neglect almost everything that doesn't lead to these remarkable and very visible short-term gains.

Identifying and Rewarding Critical Managerial Skills

Unfortunately, middle managers quickly get the message that it is important to get a running start and they may, therefore, not learn as much in the marketplace as there is to be learned (which would better shape the product) or perfect the technology as much as it could be perfected—including the process as well as the product technology.

The measurement and reward systems should be used to alleviate some of the more destructive consequences of the necessary emphasis on fast growth in venture development. This would mean, for instance, rewarding accomplishments in the areas of problem finding, problem solving, and know-how development. Success in developing the administrative aspects of the emerging venture organization should also be included, as well as effectiveness in managing the interfaces with the operating divisions.

At the operational level, where some managerial failures are virtually unavoidable, top management should create a reasonably foolproof safety net. Product champions at this level should not have to feel that running the business is the only possible reward for getting it started. Systematic search for and screening of potential venture managers should make it easier to provide a successor for the product champion *in time*. Avenues for recycling product champions/venture managers should be developed and/or their reentry into the mainstream business facilitated.

More flexible systems for measuring and rewarding performance should accompany the greater flexibility in structuring the venture-corporate relations mentioned earlier. This would mean greater reliance on negotiation processes between the firm and its entrepreneurs. To make such processes symmetrical (and more acceptable to the nonentrepreneurial participants in the organization), the internal entrepreneurs should be required to substitute negotiated for regular salary and benefits (see chapter 11).

Parenthetically we should note that a number of large corporations are beginning to devise schemes by which venture managers can get something approximating an equity interest in their new venture and thus share in the profits (and losses) they create. Control Data Corporation, for instance, has done this with respect to its ETA venture (for its new generation of supercomputers). General Motors is issuing new classes of stock to motivate the management of its newly acquired Electronic Data System Corporation unit.

There is another serious problem beyond the temptation to neglect new-product diversity and the management infrastructure; there is also misidentification of successful managers. In the field of innovation, problem-solving ability, initiative, quickness, and the ability to improvise and maintain the support of a wide circle of groups and users—all inputs—are more important measures of performance than outputs. The continuous bias toward evaluating short-term outputs in an arena in which management wants to encourage long-run development is highly counterproductive. Good managers may well be ignored or induced to go to those excesses that get "brownie points" but are, in fact, counterproductive for long-run growth.

As part of the same line of thought, the innovation process emphasizes the crucial and often undervalued role of intermediaries, managers, and technical people who can live and participate in several worlds. Management needs ways of identifying and rewarding individuals with these skills so they become an integral part of the organization. Innovations are spawned by technically trained personnel who can integrate new technical breakthroughs occurring in company laboratories with new knowledge and discipline trends that originate in the world of science and engineering. These same "in-the-middle" people or their colleagues also have to be able to bridge the world of the user and the world of the producer—to go back and forth from what is feasible to what is useful or in demand. In general, too high a premium is placed on people who advance their careers by becoming more and more specialized and compartmentalized and too little recognition is given to those who can bring together interrelated fields and interest groups.[8]

Conclusion: There Are No Panaceas

Some of the problems of learning to manage entrepreneurial activities in the context of large, diversified organizations are, in fact, general managerial problems. But these are the ones most poorly understood, perhaps because they are contrary to the simplistic and purely rational models of decision-making. The problems we observed revolved around vicious circles and managerial dilemmas, in part because managerial controls are not well designed to help top management comprehend what is really happening. Instead they often induce or seduce managers to do things that are helpful in the short run but destructive in the longer run. Also much of what is successful in countering these vicious circles and dilemmas represents *balancing* managerial actions—some of this and some of that—in contrast to consistent managerial patterns.

Thus, middle managers must learn to both bolster entrepreneurs and yet affirm the latter's independence, while at the same time asking them probing questions. Business-oriented-managers need to acquire the knowledge and technical depth to be respected by R&D professionals and to ask them meaningful questions, yet avoid getting bogged down in these or seeking to second-guess the experts. The product champion can be a somewhat unorthodox, even prima donna-ish "star" but he or she also needs to learn to work with, not in spite of, the larger organization.

Working with new-product innovation is the supreme test of good management simply because there are no comforting routines, but fortunately innovation frequently allows, and even requires the kind of individual initiative and responsibility that causes many highly talented people to give their best and accomplish extraordinary feats.

This chapter, then, proposes that managers can make ICV strategy work better by using the insights obtained from conceptualizing the managerial activities involved in ICV in terms of process models. This is so because the process model approach allows the managers involved to think through how their strategic situation relates to the strategic situation of managers at different levels who are simultaneously involved in the process. Understanding the interplay of these different strategic situations allows managers to see the relationships between problems that might otherwise remain unanticipated and seemingly unrelated. This may help them perform better as *individ-*

ual strategists while also enhancing the *corporate* strategy-making process.

Following these recommendations should result in better use of the individual entrepreneurial resources of the corporation, and thereby in an improvement of the corporate entrepreneurial capability. However, the implication is not that this process can or should become a planned one, or that the discontinuities associated with entrepreneurial activity can be avoided. ICV is likely to remain an uncomfortable process for the large, complex organization. This is so because ICV upsets the organization's carefully evolved routines and planning mechanisms, threatens its internal equilibrium of interests, and requires that the firm revise the image it has of itself. The success of radical innovations, however, is ultimately dependent on whether they can become institutionalized. This may well prove the most important challenge for managers of large, established firms in the 1980s.

CHAPTER 11

The Role of Corporate Entrepreneurship in Established Firms

In the preceding chapters, we have provided a description and conceptualization of the complete ICV process in large, diversified firms. We have discussed the strategic and administrative problems associated with the use of the new-venture division in such firms. We have also suggested recommendations that, we believe, can help such firms make their IVC strategy work better.

Yet, some may ask why firms should engage in ICV in the first place, if it is so difficult to do it well. Indeed, various authors have argued that firms should maintain the "common thread"[1] and should "stick to their knitting."[2] We believe that this may be good advice for firms that have not sufficiently exploited the incremental opportunities in their mainstream business *and* for whom these incremental opportunities are sufficient to sustain a desired growth rate. Such advice, however, assumes that the fundamental problem of an eventual decrease in incremental opportunities will not arise, and offers little information on how firms could improve their capacity to engage in *corporate entrepreneurship*—that is, extending the firm's domain of competence and corresponding set of opportunities through internally generated new combinations of resources.[3]

In the light of the received theory of strategy and organization, the term "corporate entrepreneurship" seems oxymoronic. One purpose of this chapter is to present a new model of strategic behavior in large, established firms that identifies entrepreneurial activity as a natural and integral part of the strategic process. This model also allows us to shed more light on why the strategic managment of such entrepreneurial activities constitutes a real challenge for corporate management. The second purpose of the chapter is to propose an analytical framework that corporate management may find useful for improving its capacity to deal effectively with entrepreneurial initiatives. This, in turn, provides the basis for discussing conditions under which various organizational designs for corporate entrepreneurship may be appropriate, and for briefly raising some issues and problems associated with implementing such designs. In particular, this conceptual framework provides a broader basis for understanding the conditions under which a new-venture division (NVD) may be an appropriate design.

A New Model of the Strategic Process

As a result of our own study of strategic decision-making regarding ICV, and of reinterpreting the data found in other major descriptive studies,[4] we feel we can propose a new model of the strategic process that is both simple and general and is useful in a discussion of the strategic management challenges associated with corporate entrepreneurship. This model is represented in Figure 11-1.

Figure 11-1 depicts two fundamentally different strategic processes going on simultaneously. We believe that the model applies especially well to large, complex firms, but may be useful for understanding the strategic management process in smaller firms too.

Induced Strategic Behavior Loop

The "bottom loop" of the model shown in Figure 11-1 corresponds to the traditional view of top-driven strategic management. The cur-

Figure 11–1

A New Model of the Strategic Process (*From "A Model of the Interaction of Strategic Behavior, Corporate Context, and the Concept of Strategy" by R. A. Burgelman*, Academy of Management Review, *8 (1), 1983, by permission of* Academy of Management Review.)

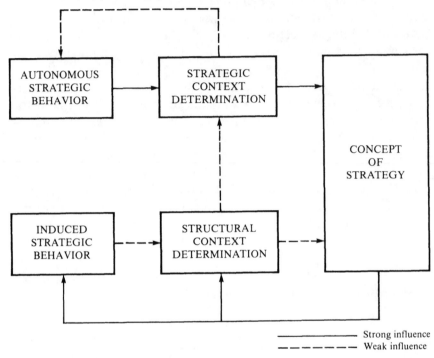

rent *concept of strategy* represents the more or less explicit articulation of the firm's theory about the basis for its past and current successes and failures. It provides a generally shared frame of reference for managers at operational and middle levels in the organization, and provides the basis for corporate objective-setting in terms of the firm's business portfolio and allocation of resources. It is important to emphasize that the concept of strategy in this model encompasses both the rational, technical/economic basis of the strategy as well as the nonrational, values/ideology components ("our way of doing things") that top management perceives to be fundamentally associated with past and current success. Hence, we believe that "strategy" and "culture" are inherently intertwined in the makeup of organizations as they exist in reality.

The concept of strategy induces strategic activity in the firm. *In-*

duced strategic behavior must be seen in the light of existing goals encompassed by the firm's strategic planning and takes place in relationship to the firm's familiar external environment. Examples of such strategic behavior emerge around, among other issues, new-product development projects for existing businesses, market development projects for existing products, and strategic capital investment projects for existing businesses.

What we have called in Chapter 9 a *structural context* aims at keeping strategic behavior at operational levels in line with the current concept of strategy. The structural context refers to the various administrative and symbolic mechanisms that top management can manipulate to influence the perceived interests of the strategic individuals at the operational and middle levels in the organization. It intervenes in the relationship between induced strategic behavior and the concept of strategy, and operates as a selection mechanism that influences the induced strategic behavior. In Chapters 7 and 8 we have discussed in some detail the functioning of the structural context at United.

The so-called "excellent companies"[5] all seem to have found *their* way of making the induced strategic behavior loop work exceedingly well. Operational and middle-level managers in these firms understand what strategic actions are required in view of the corporate development needs, even though there may be very little explicit attention given to formal "strategy." Managers in such companies identify with the corporate ways and means, yet maintain an element of creative independence. Marks and Spencer, 3M, and Hewlett-Packard (HP) are examples of excellent *implicit* (culture-based) management of the induced strategic behavior loop. General Electric with its strategic business unit (SBU) system and, until recently, Texas Instruments with its objectives-strategies-tactics (OST) system, are examples of companies with excellent *explicit* (planning-based) management of the induced strategic behavior loop.

Autonomous Strategic Behavior Loop

During any given period of time, the bulk of strategic activity in large, complex firms is likely to be of the induced variety. The present model, however, proposes that large, resource-rich firms (like United) are likely to possess a reservoir of entrepreneurial potential at operational levels that will express itself in autonomous strategic initiatives. *Autonomous* strategic behavior introduces new categories for the definition of opportunities. Entrepreneurial participants, at the product/market level, conceive new business opportunities, engage in product championing efforts to mobilize corporate resources for these new opportunities, and perform "strategic forcing" efforts to create momentum for the further development of these new ideas. Middle-level managers attempt to formulate broader strategies for areas of new-business activity by performing "strategic building" efforts, and try to convince top management to support these schemes. These are of course, the types of strategic behaviors encountered in our study of ICV which we have discussed in the preceding chapters. Such autonomous strategic initiatives constitute an attempt to escape the selective effects of the current structural context, and they make the current concept of corporate strategy problematical. They lead to redefining the corporation's relevant environment and to broadening the scope of its business portfolio.

Autonomous strategic behavior takes shape outside the current concept of strategy. Yet, to be successful, it needs eventually to be accepted by the organization and to be integrated into its concept of strategy. The process through which this can be achieved has been identified in Chapter 9 as the process of *strategic context determination*. Strategic context determination intervenes in the relationship between autonomous strategic behavior and the concept of strategy. It encompasses the activities by means of which middle-level managers question the current concept of strategy and provide top management with the opportunity to retroactively rationalize the formulation and accomplishment of successful autonomous strategic behavior. This, in turn, changes the basis for the further inducement of strategic behavior.

The autonomous strategic behavior loop in the model reflects our findings, discussed in previous chapters, that corporate entrepreneurship typically is constituted by the interlocking strategic activities of managers at multiple levels in the firm's organizational structure. The complete model provides a theoretical context for two important findings from the literature on innovation in organizations: first, different processes are involved in *generating* and *exploiting* business opportunities[6]; and second, there may be a conflict between being excellent at incremental innovation and being capable of more radical innovation.[7] It also provides a theoretical explanation for the seemingly contradictory findings of Peters and Waterman[8] that excellent companies seem to have *both* an extraordinarily strong CEO whose influence pervades the entire organization *and* independent mavericks who engage in activities outside the regular channels of hierarchical decision-making.

The Managerial Challenge Posed by Autonomous Strategic Behavior

Consider the following examples:

> In 1966, calculators were largely mechanized; a young man working for one of the calculator companies brought to HP a model for an electronic calculator. His own firm was not interested in it because they didn't have the electronic capability. In spite of unfavorable market research forecasts, Bill Hewlett personally championed the project.[9]

> Back in 1980, a manager in Hewlett-Packard Co.'s labs tried to persuade the company's new product people to get into biotechnology. "I was laughed out of the room," says Sam H. Eletr. But venture capitalists didn't laugh. They persuaded Mr. Eletr to quit Hewlett-Packard and staked him to $5.2 million to start a new company. Its product: gene machines, which make DNA, the basic material of the genetic code—and the essential raw material in the burgeoning business of genetic engineering. Now, three years later, Hewlett-Packard has formed a joint venture with Genentech Inc. to develop tools for biotechnology. One product it is considering: gene machines.[10]

How should corporate management deal with such autonomous strategic behavior? Clearly, not every new idea or proposal can or should be adopted and developed. Yet, it is not a gratuitous exercise in Monday morning quarterbacking to ask whether the managements of the firms involved in the above-mentioned examples had made a *strategic* analysis of the proposals and whether they did, indeed, make a *strategic* decision not to pursue the proposals of their internal entrepreneurs.

From a strategic management perspective, it does not seem adequate to reject the electronic calculator because "we don't have an electronics capability" or to reject the gene-making machine because "we are not currently interested in biotechnology." It seems likely that there must have been some important relevant *capabilities* in each firm that allowed the internal entrepreneurs to come up with the proposal and perhaps even develop a prototype in the first place! Even if there was no apparent significant relationship with current capabilities and skills, it was still important to consider the *strategic opportunities and/or threats* potentially implied by the entrepreneurial proposal. It is precisely these efforts to extend the firm's domain of competence, to elaborate and recombine the current capabilities, and to define new, unanticipated opportunities that make internal entrepreneurial activity a vital part of the strategic process in large, established firms.

From a strategic management perspective, the problem is *how* corporate management can improve its capacity to deal with autonomous strategic behavior, given that, by definition, such behavior does not fit with the current corporate strategy. In the remainder of this chapter an analytical framework is proposed which can be used by corporate management to assess entrepreneurial proposals and which also leads to tentative conclusions about the use of various alternatives in organizational design for structuring the relationships between entrepreneurial initiatives and the corporate context in which they occur.

A Framework for Assessing Internal Entrepreneurial Proposals

The conceptual framework we propose focuses on two key dimensions of strategic decision-making concerning internal entrepreneurial intitiatives. One of these deals with the expected *strategic importance* of these proposals for corporate development. The other deals with the degree to which such initiatives are related to the core capabilities of the corporation, that is, their *operational relatedness*.

Assessing Strategic Importance

How is one to assess as accurately as possible the strategic importance of an entrepreneurial initiative? Even though this is clearly a most important responsibility on the part of top management, it is also, paradoxically, one for which top management is often not well equipped. Corporate-level managers in large, diversified firms tend to rise through the ranks, having earned their reputations as the head of one or more of the operating divisions. By the time they reach the top management level, they have developed a highly reliable frame of reference to evaluate business strategies and resource allocation proposals pertaining to the main lines of business of the corporation. By the same token, their substantive knowledge of new technologies and markets is limited.[11]

There is a tendency for top management to rely on corporate staffs, consultants, and informal interactions with peers from other companies to make assessments of new business fields. Meritorious as such information sources may be, they are no substitute for efforts to understand the deeper substantive issues involved in a specific proposal. As we noted in Chapter 10, the latter efforts should be based on requiring middle-level managers to "educate" corporate management and encouraging middle-level managers to champion new proposals based on their own substantive assessments. Such *substantive* interaction between different levels of management is likely to improve top management's capacity to make strategically sound assessments, allowing them to rely less on purely quantitative projections.

It would seem useful for top management to have a checklist of critical issues and questions to be answered in these substantive interactions. Examples of these are:

- How does this initiative maintain our capacity to move in areas where major current or potential competitors might move?
- How does this help us to find out where *not* to go?
- How does it help us create new and defensible niches?
- How does it help mobilize the organization?
- To what extent could it put the firm at risk?
- When should we get out of it if it does not seem to be working?
- What is missing in our analysis?

Strategic assessment will sometimes result in a classification of a proposal as "very" or "not at all" important. In other cases, the situation will be more ambiguous and this will be reflected in assessments such as "important for the time being" or "maybe important in the future." Crucial to the usefulness of the analysis is that such assessments are based on specific, substantive factors.

Assessing strategic importance involves considering the opportunities and threats implied by the entrepreneurial proposal. For instance, in the earlier-mentioned example concerning Hewlett-Packard, the assessment of strategic importance would address the

177

question (among others) of whether *not* pursuing the proposal might prevent the corporation from moving into an important new area of electronic instrumentation in the future. This assessment would sharpen the understanding of the trade-offs involved in pursuing strategically related current opportunities rather than those in the emerging bioelectronics area.

Assessing Operational Relatedness

A second key dimension concerns the *degree* to which the entrepreneurial proposal requires capabilities and skills that are different from the core capabilities and skills of the corporation. This is relevant for a number of reasons. First, new-business proposals may be driven by newly developed capabilities and skills or they may drive the development of new capabilities and skills.[12] Second, entrepreneurial proposals typically are based on new combinations of corporate capabilities, and these may reveal potential opportunities for positive synergies (or the threat of negative synergies). Often, indeed, internal entrepreneurs weave together pieces of technology and knowledge that exist in separate parts of the organization and that would otherwise remain unused.

In order to be able to make the required assessments of the dimension of operational relatedness, corporate management should rely on substantive interactions with middle-level managers championing entrepreneurial projects. To guide these interactions, corporate management needs again to draw up a checklist of critical issues and questions that must be addressed in these substantive interactions. Here are some examples:

- What are the key capabilities required to make this project successful?
- Where, how, and when are we going to get them if we don't have them yet, and at what cost?
- Who else might be able to do this, perhaps better?
- How will these new capabilities affect the capacities currently employed in our mainstream business?
- What other areas may possibly require successful innovative efforts if we move forward with this project?

• What additional new things may we be able to do if we can learn to handle this project?
• What is missing in our analysis?

A useful tool to help corporate management with this assessment is to develop an accurate inventory of current capabilities and skills in various functional areas and to spell out in detail how each area of business activity uses these capabilities and skills. Such a capabilities/business areas inventory should be regularly updated and should provide a reference frame for each new entrepreneurial proposal. In light of this inventory, new proposals will sometimes be classified as "very" or "not at all" related. In other cases, the situation will be again somewhat unclear, and this may lead to a "partly related" assessment. In the context of this inventory, these assessments should be made in specific, substantive terms for each proposal.

Assessing operational relatedness thus involves examining the implications of the proposal for future corporate capabilities. For instance, in the Hewlett-Packard situation, this might lead to addressing the question of whether the capabilities demonstrated by the entrepreneurial initiative reveal new areas that the firm might want to develop further to take advantage of latent technology-based synergies. Bioelectronics could be such an area for a company like Hewlett-Packard.

The assessment framework can now be used to discuss the use of various organizational design alternatives appropriate to the different types of entrepreneurial proposals.

Design Alternatives for Corporate Entrepreneurship

Having assessed an entrepreneurial proposal in terms of its strategic importance and operational relatedness, corporate management must choose an organization design for structuring the relationship between the new business and the corporation which is commensurate with the proposal's position in the assessment framework. This involves various combinations of *administrative* and *operational* linkages. Figure 11-2 shows how the administrative and operational linkages relate to the two key assessment dimensions.

179

Figure 11–2
Toward an Assessment Framework: Key Dimensions and Their Implications

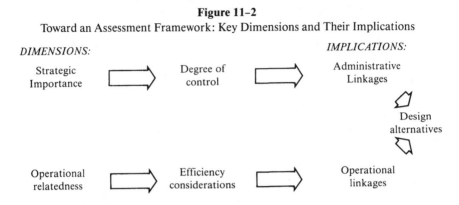

Determining Administrative Linkages

The assessment of strategic importance has implications for the degree of *control* corporate management needs to maintain over the new-business development. The premise is that firms, like individuals, will want to be able to exert control over those events and circumstances that are likely to affect their strategic positions and thus their freedom to move and pursue their own objectives. This, in turn, has implications for the administrative linkages to be established. Figure 11–3 provides some examples of administrative linkages.

If strategic importance is high, strong administrative linkages will be in order. This means, basically, that the new business must be incorporated into the existing structural context of the firm. Corporate management will want a say in the strategic management of the new business through direct reporting relationships, substantive involvement in planning/budgeting processes, and involvement in trade-offs between the strategic concerns of the new and existing businesses. Measurement and reward systems must reflect clearly articulated strategic objectives for the development of the new business. If the strategic importance of the new business is low, on the other hand, this should lead corporate management to examine how the new business can best be "spun off."

In more ambiguous situations, where strategic importance is judged to be somewhat unclear as yet, corporate management should loosen the administrative linkages and allow some leeway in the strategic management of the new business. The internal corporate venturing (ICV) activities documented in the earlier chapters of this book often seemed to be characterized by such ambiguity. In such sit-

Figure 11-3
Administrative Linkages (Examples)

HOW DEEPLY SHOULD CORPORATE MANAGEMENT GET INVOLVED IN
THE STRATEGIC MANAGEMENT OF THE ENTREPRENEURIAL BUSINESS?

1. SETTING STRATEGIC OBJECTIVES

Integrated in corporate strategic planning	←——————————→	Allowed to develop their own

2. INVOLVEMENT IN RESOURCE ALLOCATION

Substantive involvement	←——————————→	Final authorization only

3. REPORTING RELATIONSHIPS

Integrated in corporate hierarchy	←——————————→	Report to separate board

4. HIRING/FIRING

Integrated with corporate policies	←——————————→	Allowed to develop their own

5. MEASUREMENT/REWARD

Integrated with corporate policies	←——————————→	Completely negotiable

uations, as we observed in Chapter 10, the strategic context of the
new business remains to be determined. This requires mechanisms
facilitating substantive interaction between middle and corporate
levels of management, and measurement and reward systems capable
of dealing with as-yet-unclear performance dimensions and strategic
objectives.

Determining Operational Linkages

The degree of operational relatedness has implications for the *efficiency* with which both the new and the existing businesses can be
managed. The premise here is that firms seek to organize their operations in a way that maximizes synergies while minimizing the cost of
transactions across organizational boundaries. This, in turn, has implications for the required operational linkages. Figure 11-4 provides
some examples of such operational linkages.

If the operational relatedness of the new and existing businesses is

Figure 11-4
Operational Linkages (Examples)

HOW STRONGLY SHOULD THE ENTREPRENEURIAL AND CORPORATE OPERATIONS BE COUPLED?

1. INTEGRATION OF WORK FLOWS

Mutual adjustment at operational level	←→	Lateral relations between operations managers	←→	Basically independent

2. FLOW OF INFORMATION AND KNOW-HOW

Personnel transfers	←→	Professional contacts	←→	Basically no exchange

judged to be high, strong coupling of their operations is probably in order. Corporate management should ensure that both new and existing capabilities and skills are used well through integration of work flows, adequate mutual adjustment between resource users through lateral relations at the operational level, and free flows of information and know-how through regular contacts between professionals in the new and existing businesses. Low operational relatedness, on the other hand, may require complete decoupling of the operations of new and existing businesses to avoid interferences and concomitant wasteful (because unnecessary) communications and negotiations.

In situations where operational relatedness is partial and not completely clear, loose operational linkages seem most adequate. The ICV activities, again, would seem to be a case in point. In such situations, the work flows of new and existing businesses should remain basically separate, and mutual adjustment should be achieved through individual integrator roles or through task force–type mechanisms, rather than directly through operational-level managers. Information and know-how flows, however, should remain as unobstructed as is practical.

Choosing Design Alternatives

Various combinations of administrative and operational linkages produce different design alternatives. These correspond to choices which corporate management has to make regarding the different situations identified in the assessment framework. Figure 11-5 shows nine such design alternatives.

Figure 11-5

Organization Designs for Corporate Entrepreneurship (© *1984 by
the Regents of the University of California. Reprinted from* California
Management Review, *xxvi (3), p. 161, by permission of the Regents.*)

DESIGN ALTERNATIVES

		VERY IMPORTANT	UNCERTAIN	NOT IMPORTANT
OPERATIONAL RELATEDNESS	UNRELATED	3. SPECIAL BUSINESS UNITS	6. INDEPENDENT BUSINESS UNITS	9. COMPLETE SPIN-OFF
	PARTLY RELATED	2. NEW-PRODUCT/ BUSINESS DEPARTMENT	5. NEW-VENTURE DIVISION	8. CONTRACTING
	STRONGLY RELATED	1. DIRECT INTEGRATION	4. "MICRO" NEW VENTURES DEPARTMENT	7. NURTURING AND CONTRACTING

STRATEGIC IMPORTANCE

The design alternatives discussed here are not exhaustive, and the
scales for the different dimensions used in the assessment framework
remain rudimentary. Much room is left for refinement through further research. By the same token, the framework represented in Figure 11-5 allows us to provide a preliminary conceptual framework
for a number of practices encountered in today's business environment.

1. *Direct integration.* High strategic importance and operational
relatedness requires strong administrative and operational linkages.
This implies, in fact, the need to integrate the new business directly
into the mainstream of the corporation. Such integration must anticipate internal resistance for reasons well documented in the literature
on organizational change. The role of "champions" who know the
workings of the current system well is likely to be important in such
situations. The need for direct integration is perhaps most likely to
occur in fairly highly integrated firms, where radical changes in product concept and/or in process technologies could threaten the overall
strategic position of the firm. An example of the need for direct integration is documented by Twiss's account of the development of
"float glass" at Pilkington Glass, Ltd.[13]

2. *New-product/business department.* High strategic importance and partial operational relatedness requires a combination of strong administrative and medium-strong operational linkages. This may be achieved by creating a separate department around an entrepreneurial project in that part (division or group) of the operating system where potential for sharing capabilities and skills is significant. Corporate management should monitor the strategic development of the project in substantive terms, and not allow it to be incorporated into the overall strategic planning of that division or group (and thus "buried"). An example in which the proposed approach might have been useful is provided by the handling of electronic fuel injection development by Bendix Corporation, one of the major, diversified automotive suppliers. Despite the firm's having been the first to develop and patent this profoundly important new technology and despite the existence of a champion in the carburetor division, management at the automotive group level did not support the development. Only after a new group-level manager took charge of the strategic management of the project and brought in additional operational capabilities and skills did the project take off, many years later.[14]

3. *Special business units.* High strategic importance and low operational relatedness may require the creation of specially dedicated new-business units. These will usually be wholly owned by the corporation. Strong administrative linkages are necessary to ensure the attainment of explicit strategic objectives within specified time horizons throughout the development process. It will often be necessary to combine and integrate some of these business units into a new operating division in the corporate structure at a later time. IBM's use of the special business unit design to enter the personal computer business is a well-known example.[15]

4. *"Micro" new-ventures department.* Uncertain strategic importance and high operational relatedness seems typical for the "peripheral" projects which are likely to emerge in the operating divisions on a rather continuous basis. For such projects, administrative linkages should be loose. The venture manager should be allowed to develop a strategy within budget and time constraints, but otherwise not be limited by current divisional or even corporate-level strategies. Operational linkages should be strong, to take advantage of the existing capabilities and skills and to facilitate transferring back newly developed ones. Norman Fast[16] has discussed a "micro" NVD design that would seem to fit the conditions specified here.

5. *New-venture division.* This design is proposed for situations of maximum ambiguity in the assessment framework. In the light of these ambiguous situations, top management is likely to want a certain degree of direct control over activities that may turn out to be of strategic importance for corporate development. Hence, they will want to keep them *internal*, at least until greater clarity concerning their strategic importance is reached. However, top management is also likely to want to protect the efficiency of the operating system. Hence, they will want to keep the new-venture activities *separate*, at least until their degree of operational relatedness becomes more clear. The NVD design has the potential to satisfy both of these top management concerns.

The NVD may serve best as a "nucleation" device. It provides a fluid internal environment for the development of projects with the potential to create major new business thrusts for the corporation, but whose strategic importance remains to be determined as the developmental process unfolds. Administrative linkages thus should be fairly loose. Middle-level managers supervising a few ventures are expected to design "middle-range" strategies for developing new fields of business: they must bring together projects that may exist in various parts of the corporation, and/or can be acquired externally, and integrate these with some of the new-venture projects they supervise, with the aim of building sizable new businesses. Operational linkages should also be fairly loose, yet be sufficiently developed to facilitate transferring back and forth relevant know-how and information concerning capabilities and skills. Long time horizons—10 to 15 years— are necessary, but ventures should not be allowed to languish. High-quality middle-level managers, as we have seen throughout this book, are crucial to making this design work.[17]

6. *Independent business units.* Uncertain strategic importance and negligible operational relatedness may make external venture arrangements attractive. Different degrees of controlling ownership with correspondingly strong board representation may provide corporate management with an acceptable level of strategic control. IBM's use of independent business units is one example where the corporation keeps complete ownership. An example of joint ownership is provided by how Bank of America has organized its venture capital business.[18]

7. *Nurturing plus contracting.* In some cases, an entrepreneurial proposal may be considered unimportant for the firm's corporate de-

velopment strategy, yet may be strongly related to its operational capabilities and skills. Such ventures will typically address "interstices" in the market[19] which may be too small for the company to serve profitably but which offer opportunities for the development of a small business. Top management may want to help such entrepreneurs spin off from the corporation and may, in fact, help such entrepreneurs set up their businesses. The corporation could also decide to obtain a minority participation in the new business. This ensures that the firm will have a known and most likely friendly competitor in those interstices and also ensures that other competitors will be excluded. There may be a basis for long-term contracting relationships in which the corporation can profitably supply the entrepreneur with some of its excess capabilities and skills. Strong operational linkages related to these contracts may facilitate transfer of new or improved skills which may be developed by the entrepreneur. Tektronix is a company that has experimented extensively with this type of approach.[20]

8. *Contracting.* The possibilities for nurturing would seem to diminish as the required capabilities and skills of the new business are less related. Yet there may still be opportunities for obtaining a minority participation and/or making profitable contracting arrangements and for learning about new or improved capabilities and skills through some form of operational linkage.

9. *Complete spin-off.* If strategic importance and operational relatedness are both low, a complete spin-off will be most appropriate. A decision based on a careful assessment of both dimensions is likely to lead to a well-founded decision from the perception of both the corporation and the internal entrepreneur. Control Data Corporation, for instance, has established an Employee Entrepreneurial Advisory Office to help clarify situations where an internal entrepreneur desires to start his or her own business.

Implementing Design Alternatives

In order to implement designs for corporate entrepreneurship effectively, three major issues and potential problems need to be considered further. First, corporate management and the internal entrepreneur should view the assessment framework as a tool to clarify—at a particular moment in time—their community of interests and interdependences and to structure a situation where both parties can benefit. Second, corporate management must establish measurement and reward systems that are capable of accommodating the different incentive requirements of different designs. Third, as the development process unfolds, new information may modify the perceived strategic importance and operational relatedness of the new venture and the established business, which may require a renegotiation of the organizational design.

To deal effectively with these implementation issues and potential problems, corporate management must recognize internal entrepreneurs as "strategists," perhaps even encouraging them to think and act as such. This is necessary because the stability of the relationship will be dependent on both parties feeling that they have achieved their individual interests to the greatest extent, given the structure of the situation. On the part of corporate management, this implies attempts to reap benefits from the entrepreneurial endeavor, but only to the extent that corporate management can provide the entrepreneur with the opportunity to be more successful than if he or she were to go it alone. In general, the higher the degree of operational relatedness (i.e., the more the internal entrepreneur is dependent on the corporation's resources) and the lower the expected strategic importance of the entrepreneurial initiative for the corporation's future development, the lower the total rewards the internal entrepreneur will be able to negotiate. Milestones should be agreed upon for reopening the negotiations as the new business evolves. This might result, for instance, in different packages of equity shares in the new business and regular employee benefits as the situation evolves.

All of this, in turn, simultaneously requires generous policies to help internal entrepreneurs, based on a sound assessment of their proposals, and unequivocal determination to protect proprietary corporate capabilities and skills vigorously.[21]

Conclusion

Until recently, the distinction made by Schumpeter[22] between entrepreneurial and administrated ("bureaucratic") economic activity could be considered adequate. However, in the light of the turbulence that characterizes the new industrial context, this distinction seems to lose much of its relevance. Large, established corporations and new, maturing firms alike are confronted with the problem of maintaining their growth, if not their existence, by exploiting to the fullest the unique resource combinations they have assembled.

Increasingly, there is an awareness that internal entrepreneurs are necessary for firms to achieve this. Like the external entrepreneur, the internal entrepreneur creates new opportunities and gives impetus to the development of new resource combinations or recombinations. As a result, new forms of economic organization—a broader array of arrangements—seem necessary.

This, in turn, requires the development of new theories of how the firm operates and a more subtle view of the role of hierarchies, contracts, and markets. The conceptual foundations of this changing perspective are currently being laid in such fields as the economics of internal organization, agency theory, the theory of legal contracts, and theories of organizational design and change. In this final chapter, a conceptual framework has been proposed to help management assess the nature of the relationships between spontaneously emerging new business proposals and the existing corporate context. The belief underlying our proposal of this framework is that a better understanding of the process of corporate entrepreneurship will facilitate the collaboration between firms and their internal entrepreneurs.

Epilogue: A New Organizational Revolution in the Making?

This book has been a half dozen years in preparation. As we look back on our efforts and attempt to put them into the context of the major changes that have occurred in the way American managers think about their organizations and their own roles within them, we would like to leave the reader with some final themes for further reflection.

Toward a Theory of Corporate Entrepreneurship

At the end of our efforts to describe some of the more complex management processes in large, established firms, we feel even more strongly than at the outset that a theory of corporate entrepreneurship is needed. As once-excellent companies lose their luster and new ones are emerging as bright new stars, it seems clear that simply looking for exemplars of success, whose practices can be readily emulated, is not a workable alternative for serious theory-building efforts.

The outlines of the theory of corporate entrepreneurship we propose are still dim. However, we believe that it will be grounded in increased understanding of the evolutionary processes of organizational learning.

In these evolutionary organizational learning processes, we believe, entrepreneurial *individuals* at the operational and middle levels will play an increasingly important role. Our book has provided some evidence of the fact that such individuals elaborate the organization's capabilities and enact the new opportunities that are associated with the elaboration efforts. In a very important sense, they help their organizations to enlarge and embroider their "knitting" rather than just sticking to the existing domains.[1]

The challenge for American business will be to integrate new theoretical insights into its strategic management practices as they become available. This challenge is real, because the Japanese (and perhaps others as well) are already aware of the need to do so.[2]

Individualism and Big Business: A New Beginning

This leads to our second theme. We feel that our inquiry into the nature of internal corporate venturing and corporate entrepreneurship provides the basis for a rather optimistic view, but, at the same time, suggests a tremendous challenge for top management of established firms.

Almost continuously, established firms hire from the best and brightest graduates the nation's educational system has to offer. Systematic surveys, as well as our own limited but direct contact with hundreds of students at two major universities, suggest that a significant number of these young professionals have entrepreneurial aspirations and are looking for something more than the job security traditionally offered by large, established firms. On the one hand, this creates a necessity for dramatic changes in the management practices of large, established firms if they want to be able to compete with glittering new firms for entrepreneurial talent. On the other hand, it suggests the existence of an enormous potential for corporate entrepreneurship ready to exert itself and to be channeled in directions beneficial to both the individual and the firm.

It is perhaps worth noting that the existence of this potential was proposed more than 20 years ago by one of the authors of this book, who critically examined the foundations for the widely asserted contradiction between "individualism" and "big business" and found them lacking.[3] Now, it seems that the time is ripe for a new integration of individualism and big business through strategies for the implementation of corporate entrepreneurship.

In view of the challenge posed by the need to integrate individualism and big business, one should perhaps be cautious with respect to the currently fashionable recommendation that a homogeneous and overly integrated "corporate culture" be created. The challenge for established firms, we believe, is not either to be well organized and to act in unison or to be creative and entrepreneurial. The real challenge, it would seem, is to be able to live with the tensions generated by both modes of action. This will require top management's exploitation of existing opportunities to the fullest (because only relatively few will be available), the generation of entirely new opportunities (because today's success is no guarantee for tomorrow), and the balancing of exploitation and generation over time (because resources are limited). Strategic management approaches will have to accomplish all three concerns simultaneously and virtually continuously.

The Corporation of the Future

Our last theme, then, concerns the evolving nature of the established firm. It seems to us that the developments currently crystallizing in American business herald an epoch-marking change. We believe the change may well be of the same magnitude as the one that occurred during the first quarter of the twentieth century, which led to the organizational innovation represented by the "divisionalized firm" as brilliantly documented in Alfred D. Chandler's landmark study on strategy and structure.[4]

The new wave of organizational innovations involves new types of arrangements between individuals and corporations. It is likely to continue to produce *new organizational forms*, spanning the entire range of combinations of markets and hierarchies[5] and involving complex, sometimes protracted *negotiation processes* between individuals and corporate entities. Such negotiation processes, we believe, will be an increasingly pervasive aspect of corporate life and an important mechanism for facilitating the earlier-mentioned new integration of individualism and big business through corporate entrepreneurship.

191

Appendix: Methodology and Research Design

A qualitative method was chosen as the best way to arrive at an encompassing view of the ICV process.[1]

Research Setting

The research was carried out in one multibillion dollar, diversified, U.S.-based high-technology firm, which we refer to as *United*. United had traditionally produced and sold various commodities in large volume, but it had also tried to diversify through the internal development of new products, processes, and systems in order to get closer to the final user or consumer and to catch a greater portion of the total value added in the chain from raw materials to end products. During the 1960s, diversification efforts were carried out within existing operating divisions, but in the early 1970s the company established a separate new-venture division (NVD).

Data Collection

Data were obtained on the functioning of the NVD. The charters of its various departments, the job descriptions of the major positions in the NVD, the reporting relationships and mechanisms of coordination, and the reward system were studied. Finally, data were also obtained on the role of the NVD in the implementation of the corporate strategy of unrelated diversification. These data describe the historical evolution of the structural context of ICV development at United before and during the research period. Figure A–1 shows the structure of United at the time of our study.

The bulk of the data were collected by studying the six major ICV projects in progress at United at the time of the research. These ranged from a case where the business objectives were still being defined to one where the venture had reached a sales volume of $35 million.

Fermentation products was a project in the earliest stage of development. The new business opportunity was still being defined and no project had been formally started. Five people from this project were interviewed, some several times, between November 1976 and August 1977.

Fiber components was a project for which a team of R&D and business people were investigating business opportunities and their technical implications. Five people in this group were interviewed between January 1977 and May 1977.

Improved plastics was a project that had reached a point where a decision was imminent as to whether the project would receive venture status and be transferred from the corporate R&D department to the venture development department of the NVD. Seven people from this project were interviewed, some several times, between February 1977 and April 1977.

Farming systems had achieved venture status, but development had been limited to the one product around which it had been initially developed. Efforts were being made to articulate a broader strategy for further development of the venture. This was achieved during the research period, and our additional project was started. Seven people were interviewed, some several times, between November 1976 and August 1977.

Environmental systems had also achieved venture status, but was

193

The Structure of United Corporation (*Reprinted from "A Process Model of Internal Corporate Venturing in the Diversified Major Firm" by R. A. Burgelman published in* Administrative Science Quarterly, *June 1983, by permission of* The Administrative Science Quarterly. *Copyright 1983 Cornell University.*)

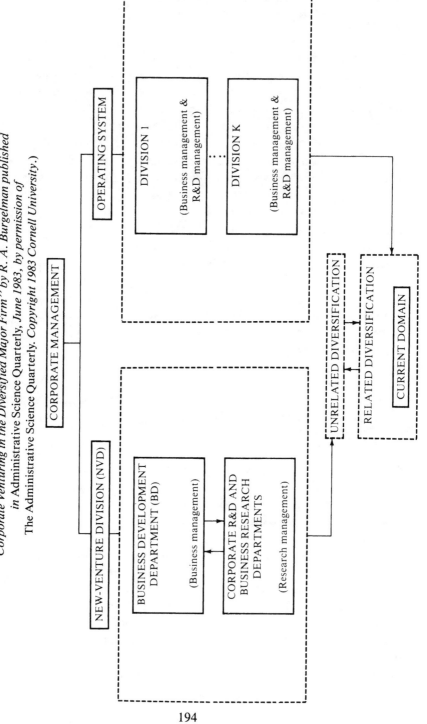

struggling to deal with the technical flaws of the product around which its initial development had taken place. It also was trying to develop a broader strategy for further development. It failed to do so, however, and the venture was halted during the research period. Six people from the project were interviewed between March 1977 and June 1977.

Medical equipment was rapidly becoming a mature new business. It had grown quickly around one major new product, but had then developed a broader strategy which allowed it to agglomerate medically related projects from other parts of the corporation and to make a number of external acquisitions. After the research period, this venture became a new free-standing division of the corporation. Eleven people from this project were interviewed, some several times, between June 1976 and September 1977.

In addition to the participants in the six ICV projects, NVD administrators, people from several operating divisions, and one person from corporate management were interviewed. A total of sixty-one people were interviewed. Table A–1 shows the distribution of persons interviewed, broken down according to job title.

The interviews were unstructured and took from one and a half to four and a half hours. Tape recordings were not made, but the interviewer took notes in shorthand. The interviewer usually began with an open-ended invitation to the interviewee to talk about work-related activities, then directed discussion toward three major aspects of the ICV development process: (1) the evolution over time of a project, (2) the involvement of different functional groups in the development process, and (3) the involvement of different hierarchical levels in the development process. Respondents were asked to link particular statements they made to statements by other respondents concerning the same issues or problems and to give examples where appropriate.

A major benefit of this approach was that it became possible to interview more people than originally planned. Respondents mentioned names of relevant individuals and were willing to help us set up interviews with them. It was thus possible to interview the relevant persons in each of the ICV cases studied and to record the convergence and divergence in their views concerning various key problems and critical situations throughout the developmental process. In some cases it was necessary to go back to a previous respondent to clarify issues or problems, and this was always possible. After com-

Table A-1

Distribution of Persons Interviewed, by Job Title

	Number
Top management of new-venture division (NVD)	
Director of NVD	2
Director of corporate R&D department	1
Director of business research department	1
Director of business development department	2
Participants from corporate R&D department	
R&D managers	4
Group leaders	10
Bench scientists	6
Participants from business research department	
Business managers	2
Business researchers	4
Participants from business development department	
Venture managers	5
Business managers	1
Technology managers	3
Group leaders in venture R&D group	3
Marketing managers	4
Marketing researchers	2
Operations managers	4
Project managers	1
Administration of NVD	
personnel managers	1
Operations managers	1
Participants from other operating divisions	
R&D managers	1
Group leaders	2
Corporate management	
Executive staff	1
Total	61

Source: Reprinted from "A Process Model of Internal Corporate Venturing in the Diversified Major Firm" by R. A. Burgelman published in *Administrative Science Quarterly*, June 1983, by permission of *The Administrative Science Quarterly*. Copyright 1983 Cornell University.

pleting an interview, the interviewer made a typewritten copy of the conversation. All in all, about 435 legal-size pages of typewritten field notes resulted from these interviews.

The research also involved the study of documents. As could be expected, the ICV project participants relied little on written procedures in their day-to-day working relationships with other participants. One key set of documents, however, was the set of written corporate long-range plans concerning the NVD and each of the ICV projects. After repeated requests, we received permission to read the plans on site and to make notes. These official descriptions of the evolution of each project between 1973 and 1977 were compared with the interview data.

Finally, occasional behavioral observations were made, for example, when other people would telephone or stop by during an interview or in informal discussions during lunch at the research site. These observations, though not systematic, led to the formulation of new questions for further interviews.

Conceptualization

The field notes were used to write a case history for each of the venture projects in which we put together the data obtained from all participants on each of the three major aspects of venture development.

This research design thus resulted in seven case histories. At the project level, the comparative analysis of the six ICV cases allowed the construction of a grounded "stages" model that described the sequence of stages and their key activities. Four stages of ICV development were identified—the conceptual, pre-venture, entrepreneurial, and organizational stages. Table A-2 shows the stages reached in each project, the number of projects observed for each stage, and the number of real-time observations of each stage.

At the corporate level, the research constituted a case study of how one diversified major firm went about ICV and how the corporate context influenced the activities in each stage of development of an ICV project. These case materials formed the basis for the conceptualization efforts presented in this book.

The major result of these conceptualization efforts is the *process model* of ICV (presented in chapter 9), which combines the project and corporate levels of analysis. Through its emphasis on the connections between strategic activities at multiple levels of management, the process model adds complexity to the discussion of ICV. Other discussions are often simpler because they limit themselves to either the organizational or the project level of analysis. The process model allows one to elucidate otherwise only vaguely perceived (and often ignored) connections between top-, middle-, and operational-level strategic action. It explicates how forces exerted by organizational-level strategy and structure interact with forces exerted by strategic behavior at the ICV project level.

Table A–2

Stages of Development Reached by Six ICV Projects

Project	Stages			
	Conceptual	Pre-venture	Entrepreneurial	Organizational
Medical equipment	*	*	*	*
Environmental systems	*	*	*	
Farming systems	*	*		
Improved plastics	*	*		
Fiber components	*	*		
Fermentation products	*			
Projects observed	6	5	3	1
Real-time observations	1	2	2	1

Note: An asterisk indicates that the project reached this stage prior to the conclusion of the study.

Source: Reprinted from "A Process Model of Internal Corporate Venturing in the Diversified Major Firm" by R. A. Burgelman published in *Administrative Science Quarterly*, June 1983, by permission of *The Administrative Science Quarterly*. Copyright 1983 Cornell University.

Additional Data and Induction

A great deal of additional data were collected from published case studies, business press accounts, and many interviews with executives in another dozen corporations. These additional data allowed for some preliminary (but of course not systematic) testing of the generalizations derived from the original field study. These data gave us the opportunity to draw conclusions from a broader array of organizations. Nevertheless, we are aware of the inherent limitations associated with the kind of research reported in this book.

Limitations of Our Study

Different research methodologies pose different problems in terms of the reliability and validity (internal and external) of the findings they produce.

Reliability of the findings is somewhat of a problem for field studies in general, since without adequate statistical testing one cannot determine how confident one can be that different researchers (or the same researcher under different circumstances) would not find significantly different results regarding the same phenomenon. In the present study, however, the use of convergence- and divergence-seeking interviews with all the key participants in the situation, and the comparison of orally obtained data with written data, would seem to minimize the risk of a systematic bias in the findings.

Internal validity is usually the greatest strength of a carefully carried out field study. The researcher's intimate familiarity with the system under study, and the generation of abundant data, coupled with the research strategy of discovering "grounded" theory provide reasonable assurance that in the present study the data and theory truly describe the ICV phenomenon.

External validity is usually a more severe problem attached to field studies in *one* setting. Bower[2] has cogently articulated the rationale for "one-observation" studies when the purpose is theory *generating* rather than theory verification:

> The kind of research needed in the study of large organizations at this stage in the evolution of knowledge is that which can inform the process of building new theory. Because critical experiments are impossible and replicating nearly so, the researcher uses the costs and benefits of the practitioner's problems as his test of relevance and validity. Large sample studies based on survey data may be undertaken, but their findings deserve no special standing. The sample is larger, but the data is weaker. At best, the result is still new insight. (p. 25)

Ultimately, the issue of external validity may be: Is the one observation representative of a broader class, or is it "idiosyncratic"? Also, it may be asked: Is the one observation not "self-selected"?

The circumstances under which the present study took place and its shape would indicate that there was no self-selection regarding the site of the study. Initial entry to the organization under study was almost accidental, and involved a lower-level participant. There was no resistance to the research, but by the same token there was no great desire for it either on the part of the corporation. Furthermore, nobody in the system (including the researcher, for that matter) knew in advance the scope and depth the research would eventually reach. These circumstances gave the researcher the opportunity to observe the system almost unobtrusively over a period of 15 months, to study what he wanted in the way he wanted, and to write up his findings without having to consult with the host organization.

As to the representativeness of the site, a few important considerations must be mentioned. It is true that the corporation was somewhat special because of the advanced concept of its NVD system which comprised the corporate R&D department as well as the new-business development department. Other research,[3] however, has indicated that some major competitors of United also had begun to reorganize their NVDs along these lines. United's approach is thus quite likely not the result of some corporate idiosyncrasies, but reflects the generic difficulties and the logic of radical innovation in large, complex business organizations.

Finally, it could be argued that the study of innovative activity in the large, complex corporation is, in fact, somewhat futile since data have suggested that much of the innovation in many industries comes from relatively small firms. The chemical and pharmaceutical industries, however, have been identified as the "exceptional cases" in this respect.[4] This of course, makes the study of a large corporation especially relevant for these industries. However, our additional data from a dozen or so other organizations and our experience in presenting our findings, conceptualizations, and recommendations to diverse managerial audiences suggest that they are quite relevant for the large, complex, high-technology corporation in general.

Notes

Preface

1. The quarterback of the Pittsburgh Steelers after helping his team win the 1979 Super Bowl, quoted in *The New York Times*, January 21, 1980, Section C.
2. Perhaps a good example is the General Electric Company. In 1983, GE's sales volume was $26.8 billion compared with 1979 when it was (in 1983 dollars) $30.8 billion. See *GE Annual Report 1983*, p. 48.

Chapter 1. Internal Corporate Venturing

1. J. J. S. Schreiber, *The American Challenge*, Atheneum Publishers, New York, 1968.
2. As Ouchi points out, the tables had already started turning in the 1960s, when American industry lost 16 percent of its share of world markets, while another 23 percent was lost during the 1970s. See W. Ouchi, *The M-Form Society*, Addison-Wesley, Reading, MA, 1984, p. 3.

3. R. Hayes and W. Abernathy, "Managing Our Way to Economic Decline," *Harvard Business Review*, 57, July–August 1980.

4. R. Reich, *The New American Frontier*, Times Books, New York, 1983.

5. W. Abernathy and J. Utterback, "Patterns of Industrial Innovation," *Technology Review*, 80, June–July 1978.

6. W. Abernathy, *The Productivity Dilemma*, Johns Hopkins, Baltimore, 1978.

7. For some examples of the problems associated with acquisitions, see "Raytheon Is Among Companies Regretting High-Tech Mergers" *Wall Street Journal*, September 10, 1984. For an example of successful acquisition strategies, see "Gould Reshapes Itself into Hi-Tech Outfit Amid Much Turmoil," *Wall Street Journal*, October 10, 1984.

8. W. Abernathy, K. Clark, and A. Kantrow, *Industrial Renaissance*, Basic Books, New York, 1983.

9. R. Hayes and S. Wheelwright, *Regaining Our Competitive Edge*, Wiley, New York, 1984.

10. P. Lawrence and D. Dyer, *Renewing American Industry*, Free Press, New York, 1983.

11. W. Ouchi, op cit.

12. T. Peters and R. Waterman, *In Search of Excellence*, Harper & Row, New York, 1982.

13. R. Kanter, *The Change Masters*, Basic Books, New York, 1983.

14. Of course, there are a wealth of contrary data. Kate Fishman, in her recent and well-researched book on the computer industry, describes Tom Watson's understandable frustration at not being able to get IBM to turn out a large computer to compete with Control Data's big machines. See K. D. Fishman, *The Computer Establishment*, Harper & Row, New York, 1981.

15. The first theoretical justification for establishing a corporate new-venture group was provided by H. I. Ansoff and R. Brandenburg in "A Language for Organizational Design: Part II," *Management Science*, 17, 1971. The abandonment of many new-venture divisions has been documented by N. Fast in *The Rise and Fall of New Venture Divisions*, UMI Research Press, Ann Arbor, MI, 1979. Still, some companies are establishing such divisions and using them effectively. See "Allied Units, Free of Red Tape, Seeks to Develop Orphan Technologies," *Wall Street Journal*, September 13, 1984. In recent years, a greater array of arrangements for carrying out a new-venture strategy have been proposed. See E. Roberts, "New Ventures for Corporate Growth," *Harvard Business Review*, 57, July–August 1980. Our point is not that new-venture departments are good or bad as such, but rather that their

establishment is only a part of the process of creating internal corporate ventures.

16. "Oops!," *Business Week*, November 8, 1984.

17. E. von Hippel, "Successful and Failing Internal Corporate Ventures: An Empirical Study and Analysis," Massachusetts Institute of Technology Working Paper 893-76, 1976. For an excellent comprehensive literature review up to 1985, see I. C. MacMillan, *Progress in Research on Corporate Venturing: 1985*, Center for Entrepreneurial Studies, New York University, New York, January 1985.

18. R. Adams, "An Approach to New Business Ventures," *Research Management*, 12, 1969.

19. R. Wallace, "New Venture Management at Owens-Illinois," *Research Management*, 12, 1969.

20. R. Peterson, "New Venture Management in a Large Company," *Harvard Business Review*, 44, May–June 1967.

21. F. Buddenhagen, *Internal Entrepreneurship as a Corporate Strategy for New Product Development*, master's thesis, Massachusetts Institute of Technology, 1967; J. Hlavacek, "Toward More Successful Venture Management," *Journal of Marketing*, 38, October 1974; K. Jones and D. Willemon, "Emerging Patterns in New Venture Management," *Research Management*, 15, 1972; K. Vesper and T. Holmdahl, "How Venture Management Fares in Innovative Companies," *Research Management*, 16, 1973.

22. E. von Hippel, An Exploratory Study of Corporate Venturing: A New Product Innovation Strategy Used By Some Major Corporations, unpublished doctoral dissertation, Carnegie-Mellon University, 1973.

23. R. Biggadike, "The Risky Business of Diversification," *Harvard Business Review*, 56, May–June 1979.

24. N. Fast, op. cit.

25. These were identified by one of the authors in his doctoral dissertation. See R. A. Burgelman, Managing Innovating Systems: A Study of the Process of Internal Corporate Venturing, unpublished doctoral dissertation, Columbia University, 1980.

26. This distinction was made by J. Schumpeter. See his classic study, *The Theory of Economic Development*, Harvard University Press, Cambridge, MA, 1934.

27. See, for instance, M. Hanan, *New Venture Management*, McGraw-Hill, New York, 1976.

28. L. Sayles, "The Innovation Process: An Organizational Analysis," *Journal of Management Studies*, 11, October 1974.

29. E. Mansfield and S. Wagner, "Organizational and Strategic Factors As-

sociated with Probabilities of Success in Industrial R&D," *Journal of Business*, 45, April 1975.

30. J. Bower, *Managing the Resource Allocation Process: A Study of Corporate Planning and Investment*, Graduate School of Business Administration, Harvard University, Boston, MA, 1970.

Chapter 2. Can Exploratory Research Be Planned?

1. James Kuhn, *Scientific and Managerial Manpower in Nuclear Industry*, Columbia University Press, New York, 1966.

2. "Searle Fights to Keep Red-Hot Aspartame Hot for a Long Time," *Wall Street Journal*, September 18, 1984.

3. J. B. Quinn, "Technological Innovation, Entrepreneurship and Strategy," *Sloan Management Review*, Spring 1979, p. 21.

4. Cf. G. Strauss, "Professionalism and Occupational Associations," *Industrial Relations*, 2, May 1963, p. 13.

5. "The Lab that Ran Away from Xerox," *Fortune*, September 5, 1983.

6. For a systematic treatment of the management of corporate R&D, see R. Rosenbloom and A. Kantrow, "The Nurturing of Corporate Research," *Harvard Business Review*, 59, January–February 1982.

7. *Wall Street Journal*, September 3, 1981.

Chapter 3. Transforming Invention into Innovation

1. The concepts of "technology push" and "need pull" were introduced by Donald Schon. See D. Schon, *Technology and Social Change*, Delacorte, New York, 1967.

2. Another recent example is from Gould, Inc. In 1981, Gould followed its successful K-100 logic analyzer with an oversophisticated and overpriced K-101 model. As one former Gould manager put it, the K-101 was a product that "only the lunatic fringe of the customer base would appreciate." See "Gould Reshapes Itself into High-Tech Outfit amid Much Turmoil," *Wall Street Journal*, October 3, 1984.

3. H. Henzler, "Functional Dogmas that Frustrate Strategy," *McKinsey Quarterly*, Winter 1982, p. 26. See also F. W. Gluck and R. N. Foster, "Managing Technological Change: A Box of Cigars for Brad," *Harvard Business Review*, 55, September–October 1978.

4. *Wall Street Journal*, September 3, 1981.

5. J. Newhouse, *The Sporty Game*, Knopf, New York, 1982.
6. *New York Times*, August 4, 1982.
7. "The Lab that Ran Away from Xerox," *Fortune*, September 5, 1983, p. 100.
8. L. R. Sayles and M. Chandler, *Managing Large Systems*, Harper & Row, New York, 1971.

Chapter 4. Conceiving New Business Opportunities

1. For other research specifically focusing on generic interface problems between R&D and marketing see, for instance, W. Souder, "Disharmony Between R&D and Marketing," *Industrial Marketing Management*, 10, 1981, pp. 67–73.
2. D. A. Schon, *Beyond the Stable State*, Norton, New York, 1971.
3. L. R. Sayles, *Managerial Behavior*, McGraw-Hill, New York, 1964.
4. The classic work on "differentiation" and "integration" issues associated with the different cognitive, emotional, and time orientations of different functional groups is P. Lawrence and J. Lorsch, *Organization and Environment*, Division of Research, Graduate School of Business Administration, Harvard University, Boston, 1967.

Chapter 5. Transforming Projects into Ventures

1. The "product champion" role was identified in previous research. See D. A. Schon, "Champions for Radical New Inventions," *Harvard Business Review*, 40, March–April 1963. Also see E. B. Roberts, "Generating Effective Corporate Innovation," *Technology Review*, October–November 1977.
2. K. D. Fishman, *The Computer Establishment*, Harper & Row, New York, 1981, p. 126.
3. Research by E. von Hippel has indicated that users can be important sources of innovation in certain industries. This happens because users adapt an existing piece of equipment to their own very specific needs and in doing so generate a new approach, a solution that is widely applicable. Hence the importance in such industries for very close relationship between market research and sales personnel of the "supplying" firm and its users. See E. von Hippel, "Users as Innovators," *Technology Review*, 80, January 1978. Also see E. von Hippel, "The Dominant

role of Users in the Scientific Innovation Process," *Research Policy*, 5, 1976.

4. The work of Tom Allen has indicated the strong effect of geographical proximity on collaboration in R&D laboratories. His work has served as an important input in the design of modern R&D facilities. See T. J. Allen, *Managing the Flow of Technology*, MIT Business Press, Cambridge, Mass., 1977.

5. The importance of the middle-level manager in ICV was already recognized by E. von Hippel in his article "Successful and Failing Internal Corporate Ventures: An Empirical Analysis," *Industrial Marketing Management*, 6, 1977. See also I. Kusiatin, "The Process and Capacity for Diversification Through Internal Development," unpublished doctoral dissertation, Harvard University, 1976; and M. A. Maidique, "Entrepreneurs, Champions, and Technological Innovation," *Sloan Management Review*, 21, Winter 1980.

Chapter 6. Establishing a One-Product Business

1. The need for strategic forcing is consistent with findings suggesting that attaining a large market share fast at the cost of early profitability is critical for venture survival. See R. Biggadike, "The Risky Business of Diversification," *Harvard Business Review*, 57, May–June 1979.

2. Economist Kenneth Arrow (1974) uses the term "salutory neglect" to denote the situation in which problems for which there are no satisfactory solutions are not placed on the agenda of the organizations. Strategic neglect, which we have observed as an independent concept in this book, has a similar meaning. Arrow points out that salutory neglect is never productive in the long run; from the perspective of the larger system this may be true, and of course the largest system will in time correct for such neglect. From the short-term perspective of the entrepreneur, however, strategic neglect of administrative issues is the necessary cost of forcing growth. See K. Arrow, *The Limits of Organizations*, Norton, New York, 1974.

3. One of the key problems encountered by Exxon Enterprises was precisely the existence of these new-product development problems in the entrepreneurial ventures (QYX, Quip, and Vydec) it had acquired and was trying to integrate. See "What's Wrong at Exxon Enterprises," *Business Week*, August 24, 1981.

4. *New York Times*, August 4, 1982. The product was an oxygen enricher for home use.

Chapter 7. From a One-Product to a Multiline Business

1. T. Kidder, *The Soul of a New Machine*, Little, Brown, Boston, 1981.
2. *Business Week*, October 3, 1983.
3. *Wall Street Journal*, December 6, 1983.
4. L. R. Sayles, *Managerial Behavior*, McGraw-Hill, New York, 1964.
5. The sociologist Max Weber has observed that organizations can continue to exist beyond the life span of their charismatic leader(s) through a process of "routinization of charisma." This process, roughly speaking, involves the development of formal procedures and routines and decision-making structures that provide permanance and stability in the organization.
6. W. J. Abernathy, *The Productivity Dilemma*, Johns Hopkins, Baltimore, 1978.
7. For a systematic study of the conflict between entrepreneurship and institutionalization, see J. R. Kimberly, "Issues in the Creation of Organizations: Initiation, Innovation, and Institutionalization," *Academy of Management Journal*, 22, 1979.

Chapter 8. The New-Venture Division in the Corporate Context

1. W. Abernathy, *The Productivity Dilemma*, Johns Hopkins, Baltimore, 1978.
2. O. E. Williamson, *Markets and Hierarchies*, Free Press, New York, 1975.
3. Ansoff and Brandenburg have observed that large, divisionalized firms often fail to take advantage of their presumably greater capabilities to engage in further diversification, because of top management's preoccupation with current businesses. To overcome this inertia, these authors suggested the creation of a separate division in the corporate structure to pursue new-business development. Following the reportedly successful experience of corporations like Minnesota Mining and Manufacturing (3M), Owens-Illinois, and DuPont, many large corporations adopted a new-venture division (NVD) during the 1970s. See H. I. Ansoff and R. G. Brandenburg, "A Language for Organization Design, Part II," *Management Science*, 17, 1971. Also see J. Hutchinson, "Evolving Organization Forms," *Columbia Journal of World Business*, Summer 1976. For some successful experiences, see R. M. Adams, "An Approach to New Business Ventures," *Research Manage-

ment, 12, 1969. R. W. Peterson, "New Venture Management in a Large Company," *Harvard Business Review*, 44, May–June 1967; and R. T. Wallace, "New Venture Management at Owens-Illinois," *Research Management*, 12, 1969. According to Eric von Hippel, autonomy from the day-to-day operations of the parent corporation; constant, visible, long-term management support; and the presence of entrepreneurial venture managers seemed to be key elements in the success of these early practitioners. See E. V. von Hippel, "Successful and Failing Internal Corporate Ventures: An Empirical Analysis," *Industrial Marketing Management*, 6, 1977.

4. Norman Fast's research has documented the precarious position of the NVD in many corporations. Based on a survey of eighteen companies that had NVDs at some point between 1965 and 1975, and on three in-depth case studies, Fast found not only that NVDs took on diverse shapes, but also that a high proportion of them were short-lived. Of the eighteen NVDs studied, nine were inoperative by 1976. Furthermore, Fast found that NVDs become inoperative in one of three ways: (1) by retaining the ventures they had started and growing into an operating division, (2) by being given a staff function, and (3) by being disbanded. He noted that most of the surviving NVDs evolved through the course of their development and that the driving forces behind such evolution were: (1) changes in the corporate strategic posture, and (2) changes in the NVDs' political posture. See N. D. Fast, "The Future of Industrial New Venture Departments," *Industrial Marketing Management*, 8, 1979.

5. The idea that entrepreneurial activity acts as insurance against environmental turbulence was first proposed by R. A. Peterson and D. G. Berger, in "Entrepreneurship in Organizations: Evidence from the Popular Music Industry," *Administrative Science Quarterly*, 16, 1971. See also R. A. Burgelman, "Corporate Entrepreneurship and Strategic Management: Insights from a Process Study," *Management Science*, 29, 1983.

Chapter 9. An Overview of Internal Corporate Venturing

1. For the first use of the "process model" approach see J. L. Bower, *Managing the Resource Allocation Process*, Graduate School of Business Administration, Harvard University, Boston, 1970. The concepts of "definition," "impetus" and "structural context" are borrowed from Bower's framework.

2. The concept of "strategic context" provides the basis for extending the process model to ICV. See R. A. Burgelman, "A Process Model of Internal Corporate Venturing in the Diversified Major Firm," *Administrative Science Quarterly*, June 1983, pp. 223–244.

3. For an additional example of the "stages of growth" model approach, see the interesting article by J. R. Galbraith, "The Stages of Growth," *Journal of Business Strategy*, 1983, pp. 70–79.

Chapter 10. Management Strategies That Improve the Odds

1. L. R. Sayles and M. Chandler, *Managing Large Systems*, Harper & Row, New York, 1971.

2. "Acquiring Without Smothering," *Fortune*, November 12, 1984.

3. One of the authors has suggested that such "organizational learning" may be an important hidden benefit of entrepreneurial activity in established firms. Hence, such benefits (if acquired) should be deducted from the cost of new-venture activities. See R. A. Burgelman, "Corporate Entrepreneurship and Strategic Management: Insights from a Process Study," *Management Science*, 29, December 1983. A parallel argument has been proposed for the new-product development process in general in M. A. Maidique and B. J. Zirger, "The Success–Failure Learning Cycle in New Product Development," unpublished research paper, School of Industrial Engineering and Engineering Management, Stanford University, Stanford, CA, 1984. The Japanese have emphasized such organizational learning all along. See K. Imai, I. Nonaka, and H. Takeuchi, "Managing the New Product Development Process: How Japanese Firms Learn and Unlearn," Discussion Paper 118, Institute of Business Research, Hitotsubashi University, Tokyo, 1984.

4. Some major industrial companies, notably DuPont and General Electric, have recently appointed CEOs with far-ranging experience concerning the innovation process in their organizations.

5. For a theoretical development of the argument, see R. A. Burgelman, "A Model of the Interaction of Strategic Behavior, Corporate Context, and the Concept of Strategy," *Academy of Management Review*, 8, 1983.

6. An overview of different forms of corporate venturing is provided in E. B. Roberts, "New Ventures for Corporate Growth," *Harvard Business Review*, 58, July–August 1980.

7. Some firms seem to have developed the position of corporate historian.

See "Historians Discover the Pitfalls of Doing the Story of a Firm," *Wall Street Journal*, December 27, 1983. Without underestimating the difficulties the occupant of such a position is likely to encounter, one can imagine the possibility of structuring it in such a way that the relevant data would be recorded. Another group, possibly a committee appointed by the Board of Directors, could periodically interpret these data along the lines suggested.

8. This is a key finding of R. Kanter, *The Change Masters*, Basic Books, New York, 1983.

Chapter 11. The Role of Corporate Entrepreneurship in Established Firms

1. H. I. Ansoff, *Corporate Strategy*, McGraw-Hill, New York, 1965.
2. T. J. Peters and R. H. Waterman, *In Search of Excellence*, Harper & Row, New York, 1983.
3. For a discussion of the theoretical foundations of corporate entrepreneurship, see R. A. Burgelman, "Corporate Entrepreneurship and Strategic Management: Insights from a Process Study," *Management Science*, 29, 1983.
4. R. A. Burgelman, "A Model of the Interaction of Strategic Behavior, Corporate Context, and the Concept of Strategy," *Academy of Management Review*, 8, 1983.
5. Peters and Waterman, op. cit.
6. J. Q. Wilson, "Innovation in Organization: Notes Toward a Theory," in J. D. Thompson (ed.), *Approaches to Organizational Design*, University of Pittsburgh Press, Pittsburgh, 1966.
7. W. Abernathy, *The Productivity Dilemma*, Johns Hopkins, Baltimore, 1978.
8. Peters and Waterman, op. cit.
9. R. M. Atherton and D. M. Crites, "Hewlett-Packard: a 1975–1978 Review," Harvard Business School Case Services, Boston, 1980.
10. "After Slow Start, Gene Machines Approach a Period of Fast Growth and Steady Profits," *Wall Street Journal*, December 13, 1983.
11. Henry Kissinger has made the interesting observation that top policymakers are, basically, strategists-in-action whose fundamental strategic premises are a given by the time they reach their positions. See H. A. Kissinger, *White House Years*, Little, Brown, Boston, 1979.
12. See A. R. Fusfeld, "How to Put Technology into Corporate Planning," *Technology Review*, 80, May 1978.

13. B. Twiss, *Managing Technological Innovation*, 2nd ed., Longman, London, 1980. See also A. C. Cooper and D. Schendel, "Strategic Responses to Technological Threats," *Business Horizons*, February 1976, for a discussion of the difficulties firms face when confronted with radical technological changes affecting their mainstream operations.

14. "Bendix Corporation (A)" 9-378-257, Harvard Business School Case Services, Boston, 1981.

15. See "Meet the New Lean, Mean IBM," *Fortune*, June 13, 1983.

16. N. D. Fast, *The Rise and Fall of Corporate New Venture Divisions*, UMI Research Press, Ann Arbor, MI, 1979.

17. For an apparently successful use of the NVD, see "Allied Unit, Free of Red Tape, Seeks to Develop Orphan Technologies." *Wall Street Journal*, September 10, 1984.

18. See *Fortune*, op. cit. And see "Despite Greater Risks, More Banks Turn to Venture-Capital Business," *Wall Street Journal*, November 28, 1983.

19. For a discussion of the concept of "interstice," see E. T. Penrose, *The Theory of the Growth of the Firm*, Blackwell, Oxford, 1968.

20. See "Tektronix New-Venture Subsidiary Brings Benefits to Parent, Spinoffs," *Wall Street Journal*, September 18, 1984.

21. For an account of some examples, see "Spin-Offs Mount in Silicon Valley," *New York Times*, January 3, 1984.

22. J. A. Schumpeter, *The Theory of Economic Development*, Harvard University Press, Cambridge, MA, 1934.

Epilogue: A New Organizational Revolution in the Making?

1. See R. A. Burgelman, "Strategy-Making and Evolutionary Theory: Towards a Capabilities-Based Perspective," Research paper series no. 755, Graduate School of Business, Stanford University, Stanford, CA, 1984.

2. This is clearly suggested by the following quote:

   > If there is a clearly defined goal, we can follow the ordinary decision process. . . . However, when the corporate goals and strategic objectives are often ambiguous, as in the present situation, the ordinary approach does not work properly. We can only take the evolutionary approach; we act first, examine the feedback, and then gradually define the goal.

   See "Business Management in the New Industrial Revolution," White Paper, Japan Committee for Economic Development, 1983, pp. 14–15.

3. L. R. Sayles, *Individualism and Big Business*, McGraw-Hill, New York, 1964.
4. A. D. Chandler, *Strategy and Structure*, MIT Press, Cambridge, MA, 1962.
5. O. E. Williamson, *Markets and Hierarchies*, Free Press, New York, 1975.

Appendix: Methodology and Research Design

1. For an in-depth discussion of the methodological foundation of our approach, see J. Glaser and A. L. Strauss, *The Discovery of Grounded Theory*, Aldine, Chicago, 1967; R. A. Nisbet, *Social Change and History*, Oxford University Press, New York, 1969; Andrew M. Pettigrew, "On Studying Organizational Cultures," *Administrative Science Quarterly* 24, 1979. Also see L. Mohr, *Explaining Organizational Behavior*, Jossey-Bass, San Francisco, 1982, especially Chapter 2.
2. J. L. Bower, *Managing the Resource Allocation Process*, Graduate School of Business, Harvard University, Boston, MA, 1970.
3. N. Fast, *The Rise and Fall of New Venture Divisions*, UMI Research Press, Ann Arbor, MI, 1979.
4. See, for instance, O. E. Williamson, *Markets and Hierarchies*, Free Press, New York, 1975, especially Chapter 10.

Index

213

216